HATE ON TRIAL

HATE ON TRIAL

THE ZUNDEL AFFAIR
THE MEDIA
PUBLIC OPINION
IN CANADA

Gabriel Weimann
and
Conrad Winn

MOSAIC PRESS
OAKVILLE NEW YORK LONDON

Canadian Cataloguing in Publication Data

Weimann, Gabriel, 1950-
Hate on trial

Bibliography: p.
Includes index.
ISBN 0-88962-328-7 (bound). - ISBN 0-88962-329-5 (pbk.)

1. Zundel, Ernst - Trials, litigation, etc. - Public opinion. 2. Trials (Hate propaganda) - Canada - Public opinion.* 3. Public opinion - Canada. 4. Mass media - Canada. I. Winn, Conrad, 1945- II. Title.

KE229.Z86W43 1986 345.71'0256 C86-093495-0

Published by Mosaic Press, P.O. Box 1032, Oakville, Ontario, L6J 5E9, Canada. Offices and warehouse at 1252 Speers Road, Unit 10, Oakville, Ontario, L6L 5N9, Canada.

Published with the assistance of the Canada Council and the Ontario Arts Council.

Design by Rita Vogel.
Typeset by Lount Graphics Ltd.
Printed and bound in Canada.

ISBN 0-88962-328-7 cloth
0-88962-329-5 paper

MOSAIC PRESS:

In the United States: Flatiron Book Distributors, 1170 Broadway, Suite 807, New York, N.Y., 10001, USA.

In the U.K: John Calder (Publishers) Ltd., 18 Brewer Street, London, W1R 4AS, England

Gabriel Weimann

Professor Weimann is an Israeli sociologist and scholar of communications. He was born in Israel in 1950, the only child of two Holocaust survivors. After four years' service in the military, he acquired his B.A. and M.A. in sociology at the University of Haifa and his Ph.D. at the Hebrew University of Jerusalem. He has written extensively in scholarly periodicals on terrorism and the media, polling campaigns and voting behaviour, informal communication, and on other topics. Senior Lecturer in Sociology at Haifa University, Dr. Weimann has received awards from several granting agencies, including the Fulbright, Ben Gurion, and Canada-Israel Academic Foundations. The book was written while he was Visiting Professor at Carleton University and at Stanford University, California. He is currently preparing a book on terrorism and the media.

Conrad Winn

Professor Winn holds a B.A. in the social sciences from McGill University and a Ph.D. in political science from the Wharton School, University of Pennsylvania. He is co-author of the books, *Political Parties in Canada* and *Broadcasting Policy and Copyright Law.* His scholarly articles have dealt with cultural policy, communications, public opinion, cabinet-public service relations, legislative behaviour, affirmative action, and other topics. He is currently preparing an introductory text in political science and an anthology on affirmative action. Dr. Winn is sponsoring editor for the Addison-Wesley Publishing Company and has been a consultant to the federal cabinet secretariat and to other Canadian and U.S. government agencies. He is currently Professor of Political Science at Carleton University.

CONTENTS

In Memory of

Rachel and Mari-Ann

and for

Peter, Danny and Tammy

Acknowledgements

We deeply appreciate the assistance which professors, journalists, clergy, students and individual citizens have offered during the course of the project.

The following students helped provide the content analysis of Canadian and foreign daily newspapers: Leroy Deslandes, Maddelena Giustiniani, Moneca Kaiser, Stephen Phillips, Michael Sheaman, Lisa Wellman, and especially Lorna V. Smith and Colleen Sullivan. Elizabeth-Ann Fauteaux's editing assistance was highly appreciated.

Data on the news and public affairs coverage of CBC television were made possible thanks to John Owen, Managing Editor, and Laura Marshall. Data from Radio Canada television were made possible thanks to André Bouchard, Assistant to the Editor-in-chief, television news.

The specially designed national public opinion poll was made possible thanks to a grant from the League for Human rights of B'nai Brith, which was in turn made possible by a grant from the Multiculturalism Directorate, Secretary of State, Government of Canada. Statistical analysis was faciliated by grants from the Dean of Social Sciences, Carleton University and the Canada-Israel Foundation for Academic Exchange.

Clara Hatton, Eric Lugtigheid, Dr. Dhiru Patel and Professor H. Taylor Buckner were helpful in the design of the questionnaire.

The following individuals were helpful in the interpretation or analysis of our findings: Professor Alan Davies, Alan Borovoy, Rev. Brian Prideaux (Anglican), Rev. William Gilbert (Anglican), Rev. Arthur F. Conrad (Lutheran), Father Brendan O'Brien, Father Cosmos Mogella, Rabbi Reuven P. Bulka (Orthodox), Professor Randal Marlin, Professor Sandra Came, and John Owen (CBC). Professors Peter Emberley, Aviva Freedman, and Steve Wilson, and Alan Shefman kindly reviewed the manuscript and offered suggestions. The two authors should be held exclusively and equally responsible for errors of fact and interpretation.

Introduction

Irving Abella

In 1967 a lonely old man died in a Montreal rooming-house. Once Canada's leading anti-Semite, Adrien Arcand had long before passed from public view; his exploits as the country's foremost fascist were largely forgotten. He died penniless and friendless, unlamented and ignored. Peculiarly, through his years of poverty he clung desperately to his most prized possession, a unique collection of anti-Jewish books, manuscripts and pamphlets.

In his will Arcand bequeathed his archive of hate to a young German emigré who had arrived in Canada some years before. A draftsman by training, the young man had sought out Arcand and developed a friendship. Clearly Arcand saw something in this German. Perhaps he reminded the elderly fascist of his younger days as a firebrand. Certainly they shared the same beliefs and aspirations. And both hated Jews. Thus it was perhaps not surprising that the aging anti-Semite should hand over his life's work to his young disciple. Symbolically, the torch had been passed to a new generation. Ernst Zundel – he dropped the "e" later on – had been given his marching orders. He promised to make good use of Arcand's infamous library.

And indeed he did. Within a decade, Zundel had become the country's most notorious anti-Semite, and North America's leading publisher of hate propaganda. By the end of the 1970s his message of hate was being spread around the world. When West German police raided the offices of various neo-Nazi organizations in 1981, to their surprise they found that the bulk of the hate materials they discovered had been published by Ernst Zundel in Toronto. At the time of his trial in 1984, the paunchy, balding Toronto publisher could boast that his material was being distributed in at least 50 countries and was translated into 15 languages.

Yet bringing this hate-monger to trial caused much division in Jewish and legal circles. Both had debated for years whether a trial was worth the cost.

As a prominent rabbi put it: "Taking on anti-Semites and Holocaust deniers in the sanctified courtroom environment is like responding to someone who calls your mother a prostitute. By defending you raise the question that maybe she really was."

Was a court the appropriate forum for dealing with the Zundels of Canada? Should the state prosecute lunatic fringe groups and expose their insanity, but while doing so give them a platform? Or should these madmen be dismissed merely as harmless cranks and their ravings go unnoticed – and, more importantly, unpunished. These arguments would continue, long after the trial.

For most Canadians the seven-week trial was a numbing, wrenching nightmare. Daily on television sets and in newspapers, the horrors of the Holocaust were recalled – worse, they were challenged. Zundel and his supporters charged that not only were there no horrors, there was no Holocaust. The hearts of all Canadians of good will went out to the survivors of the death camps, especially to those in the courtroom who were put through a new and invidious torture by Zundel's lawyer. They had to prove to the world that what happened to them really happened, that events too horrible to be believed were not too horrible to have taken place.

Whether the trial of Ernst Zundel was strategically wise or not is debatable. What is not debatable is that it provided a salutory lesson. It allowed Canadians – many for the first time – to confront the menacing and ugly face of hate head-on. People capable of lying about the Holocaust, are capable of anything. It introduced Canadians into the nether world of bigots and racists. Lies that go unchallenged, the Nazis taught us, may be mistaken for truths; they may become policies and ultimately murders. As a noted theologian warned: "Of all the organs in the body, the tongue is the most dangerous."

Fifty years ago the world was divided into two parts – those places where Jews could not live, and those, like Canada where they could not enter. A generation ago, the nations of the world were put to the test of civilization, and they failed ignominiously. Though the Nazis planned and executed the Holocaust it was made possible because of the apathy of the Western world. No nation was prepared to open its doors to save Jews; none made the Jewish plight a priority. Rescue required sanctuary and there was none; it required concern where there was only indifference; it required committment where there was hostility.

We live in a far different society today; yet again, in front of a largely indifferent world Jews struggle for their very existence. Both their future and their past are questioned. There are those who would deny Jews their future by advocating the destruction of the State of Israel and by equating

Zionism with racism. And there are those who would deny Jews their past by denying the Holocaust. And in the Zundels of the world these two streams merge. Jews, they say, have no future, because they have no past. This is the new invidious anti-Semitism of the 1980's. Those who control the past, George Orwell cautioned, control the future, and those who distort Jewish history, and question the Holocaust, create the conditions for the denial of Jewish existence. That is why this book is so profoundly important.

It is not about Zundel, nor is it about his trial. Rather it is about the people of Canada; it is about our journalists, our educators, our ministers, our politicians. In a significant sense, it is about Canadian society in the 1980s, and how it reacted to the infamies in the Toronto courtroom.

Professors Weimann and Winn have performed an admirable service to their nation. With the help of an army of students, researchers and pollsters they have told us more about ourselves than many Canadians cared to know. They have gauged the levels of tolerance and prejudice in Canadian society – and they have done it objectively and analytically. They have provided us with the answers to those questions we were so concerned over about during the trial.

Was it right to charge Zundel? Did the trial increase anti-Semitism in Canada? Did it raise doubt about the Holocaust? How influential is the media? Did it pay too much attention to the trial? Who listened? How extensive is anti-Semitism? In what parts of the country and amongst what sort of people and religious groups is it a problem?

The answers to these questions are troubling, yet at the same time reassuring. No Canadian can read this book without gaining new insights into the country of which he is a part. Those of us who have written or spoken about anti-Semitism and racism have done so largely from documentary and anecdotal evidence. Weimann and Winn provide us for the first time with hard, factual, unimpeachable scientific data. Their polling will make an inestimable contribution to our understanding of the nature of Canadian society. This book is a landmark in the study of prejudice and racism in Canada.

November, 1985

Chapter 1

The Zundel Affair

Background to the Case

A German citizen and landed immigrant in Canada, Ernst Zundel operated for years a publishing enterprise from his home in Toronto's Cabbagetown area. During the 1970's, he earned his living mainly as a photo-retoucher and picture-framer. Publishing was just a sideline. But, publishing gradually occupied more and more of his time until it became his principal activity.

His home included concrete fortifications, duplicating equipment for his many pamphlets, living space for his followers, and a camera to videotape visitors. The basement contained his pride and joy, a detailed scale model of the Auschwitz death camps. Zundel was fond of telling people that the scale model was essential for his "scientific" research and for his efforts to demonstrate that gassing did not occur.[1] His duplicating equipment enabled him to manufacture propaganda booklets extolling the Third Reich and Nazi ideals. These pamphlets were exported to 42 countries around the world, including West Germany, Sweden, and other jurisdictions in which their manufacture was restricted.[2]

Zundel's trial was held in Toronto in early 1985. On February 28th, a panel of twelve ordinary Canadians reached a verdict. The accused was convicted on one count of transgressing Section 177 of the Criminal Code of Canada. According to this longstanding and rarely used provison, "every one who wilfully publishes a statement, tale or news that he knows is false and that causes or is likely to cause injury or mischief to a public interest is guilty of an indictable offense and is liable to imprisonment for two years." On March 25th, Ernst Zundel was sentenced to 15 months in prison. After a hearing in May, Zundel was ordered deported. By autumn, his deportation order was in the process of being carried out.

Less than six weeks after Zundel's conviction, James Keegstra was brought to trial under a different section of the Criminal Code. Keegstra, who testified for the defence in the Zundel trial, was a high school history teacher in Eckville, Alberta until January, 1984, when he was dismissed for unprofessional conduct. For twelve years, he indoctrinated his students with Jewish conspiracy explanations of history. His teaching included a denial of the historical facts of the Holocaust. An Alberta court sentenced Keegstra to five months in jail and a fine of $5000 for the "willful promotion of hatred against Jews."

Other hate trials may take place in the years to come. In New Brunswick, a private citizen has been urging the provincial government to prosecute a publisher of hate propaganda under the Criminal Code.[3] If other trials do take place, the Zundel trial will come to be viewed as the first in a series rather than a unique event. Whether the Zundel trial was a uniqe event or the first in a series, it was a very special event. The trial elicited an enormous amount of media attention. The defendant wanted it that way.

The Ontario Attorney General's office charged Zundel under section 177 of the Criminal Code because a Toronto lady, Sabina Citron, swore out a complaint against him under that section in 1983. A survivor of the death camps, Mrs. Citron and fellow members of the Canadian Holocaust Rememberance Association were concerned for years about the growth of hate propaganda in Canada. As Australia, Britain, Germany, Sweden and other countries enacted new laws or applied existing ones against hate literature, Canada gradually became a more important centre for the production of such works.

Sabina Citron had been active in the Holocaust committee of the Canadian Jewish Congress until 1978, when the two parted ways over the issue. The long established, respected Canadian Jewish Congress was cautious over the issue. It did not want to provide a platform for Nazis and it did not want to risk provoking a backlash. According to the irrepressible Mrs. Citron, it was simply a case of "some bad (Jewish) leaders:" "Zundel's publications are hate propaganda and we don't have to tolerate it." According to the lady, Jews who are afraid to expose Zundel have a "galut" or diaspora mentality – they are willing to bow to any demand or persecution.[4]

Somewhere between the cautiousness of the Jewish Congress and the impatience of the Rememberance Association fell the League for Human Rights of B'nai Brith. Zundel was prosecuted and convicted under a section of the Criminal Code which outlaws the publication of false news against the public interest. Like the Canadian Jewish Congress, the B'nai Brith League wanted him charged under the hate propaganda section instead. Zundel was charged under the false news section (section 177) because prosecution under this section did not need the Attorney-General's consent. Prosecution under the hate propaganda section (281.2) needed the Attorney-General's approval.

Ontario's Attorney-General would not give his approval. He feared that the federal hate law was so badly drafted, so full of loopholes, that the devil himself would be found not guilty.[5] In September, 1983, the League for Human Rights began a lobbying effort to persuade the federal Minister of Justice to remove loopholes in the law so that provincial Attorneys-General would be more willing to use it.

The actual charge against Zundel was based on two booklets, *The West, War, and Islam* and *Did Six Million Really Die?*. Zundel published both while authoring only the former. The latter was a classic example of Holocaust denial literature. The authors of Holocaust denial literature describe themselves as "revisionists." The pamphlet simply stated that the Holocaust had never taken place. The myth of the Holocaust was fabricated by a Jewish conspiracy whose purpose was to extort money from the West German government and political support from Western countries.

The pamphlet, *The West, War, and Islam,* belonged to the genre of anti-Jewish writing known as the "new anti-Semitism." The "new" anti-Semitism employs anti-Zionism as a cloak for traditional anti-Jewish hate. Zionists are sometimes contrasted with Jews. Zionists are portrayed as militarists, racists, and manipulators of public opinion while Jews are nonpolitical and keep their religious beliefs to themselves. The new anti-Semites sometimes indicate that they are not anti-Jewish, only anti-Zionist. Jews may be tolerable so long as they do not inhabit Israel and feel no affection for the country.[6]

Zundel's pamphlet, *The West, War and Islam,* lacked the subtle qualifier that Jews may be acceptable if they would only repudiate Zionism. A passage from the pamphlet spoke of "vicious, greedy and militant people who call themselves 'Jews' . . . as 'God's Chosen People.' Ever since 1945, the Zionists and their hirelings have used their self-serving myth as a tool for the deception of the Western Christian masses . . . Western Christians have become circumcised mentally and physically."[7]

Zundel's two pamphlets reflected a world view which he would articulate whenever he was given an opportunity. To whomever would listen, Zundel insisted that the mountains of evidence about the existence of the Holocaust were bogus. When a student reporter pointed to *The Diary of Anne Frank* as evidence, Zundel insisted that it was a fraud. Zundel claimed that West German forensic experts had proven that it was written in 1951 and in ball-point pen, a post-war invention. Hence, Anne had to have survived the war.[8] Zundel did not explain how the diary could have been written in 1951 in view of the fact that it was first published in 1947. Nor did he attempt to explain away the considerable documentary evidence that the fifteen year old girl was shipped to her death in 1944.

A prolific writer and publisher, Zundel espoused not only Holocaust denial and anti-Zionism, but Nazism as well. Writing under a pen name, Christof Frederich (his middle names), Zundel co-authored *The Hitler We Loved and Why,* a book published in the United States by White Power Publications. The book referred to the Fuhrer as "this humble, totally dedicated savior. . . We love him still." A photograph featured the Rev. Martin Luther King receiving an award from Rabbi Jacob Rothschild with the caption "The Face of the Enemy." Zundel rarely suppressed his enthusiasm for Hitler. During the trial, Zundel told an interviewer that the Fuhrer was "the democrats' democrat . . . the Abraham Lincoln of Germany."[9]

Zundel and Keegstra were closely linked to an extremist network coordinated by Willis A. Carto. A one-time organizer for the John Birch Society, Carto established the racist Liberty Lobby in Washington in 1961. In California, he created the Institute for Historical Review, the leading source of Holocaust denial literature. Calling history books on the Holocaust "atrocity propaganda," the Institute offered a $50,000 award to anyone who could provide evidence that the event took place. The publicity effort boomeranged when a survivor of the death camps actually applied for the award. In July, 1985, lawyers for the Institute for Historical Review hurried to reach a financial settlement with the survivor before the case could reach the courts.

Under various organizational guises, Willis Carto published a number of different periodicals and books. One periodical, *Western Destiny,* extoled the Nordic mystique. A 600 page book, *Imperium,* bemoaned the threat to civilization posed by humanism, capitalism, and democracy. It warned against Black and other "culture distorters" spawned by the "church, state, nation, race of the Jews." In a November, 1982 issue of his periodical, *Spotlight,* Carto wrote that the Korean, Viet-Nam and 1939-45 wars all took place because of the "triple-headed bloody beast" of international capitalism, international communism, and international political zionism. Elsewhere, Carto wrote that "Hitler's defeat was a defeat of Europe and America." International Jews had blinded the West. Instead of being the victims of World War II, Jews were the master manipulators of the conflagration. Using a theme with a medieval pedigree, Carto declared that Jews were so bad that Satan himself may have invented them.[10]

Holocaust Denial in Historical Perspective

There is a considerable history to the idea that Jews are not really victims, but master conspirators who pretend to be victims for machiavellian reasons. The modern roots of the idea of Jew as master manipulator lie in the book, *Protocols of the Elders of Zion.* As Europe encountered the growing pains of urbanization, industrialization, and secularism, conspiracy theories abounded. Among Catholic countries, conspiracy theories often involved Free Masons. Among Protestant countries, conspiracies were allegedly masterminded by a secret sect of Jesuit priests. Among both Catholic and Protestant countries, conspiracy theories often featured Jews in league with the devil. Medieval art often portrayed Jews and the devil as having the same features. For example, both were thought to have red hair. The medieval fantasy of a Jewish/demonic conspiracy against Christendom has been called "a warrant for genocide."[11] The *Protocols of the Elders of Zion* was a widely read document which allegedly proved the existence of an international Jewish conspiracy.

A fraud first manufactured and distributed by the Czarist secret police in about the year 1900, the *Protocols* was presented as evidence that Jewish leaders from around the globe met in Switzerland in secret to plot the financial and political exploitation of the world. The *Protocols* were supposedly the minutes of such a meeting. In fact, the *Protocols* were largely plagiarized from a French political satire of Napoleon III which was not concerned with Jews.[12] During the dying days of the Czarist regime, the *Protocols* were widely disseminated in an attempt to persuade Russians to hold Jews rather than the regime itself responsible for the regime's failures and the people's misfortunes.

Beginning in the late 19th century, Europeans who were anti-Jewish began calling themselves "anti-Semites." Self-styled anti-Semitic political parties flourished in cental Europe in the late 1920's and 1930's. Pseudo-genetic writing by French Count Arthur de Gobineau inspired the new term. In his *Essay on the Inequality of Human Races* (circa 1852), Gobineau warned that Europe could only remain proud if it remained racially pure. "Nordic-Aryan" Europe would degenerate if it permitted itself to be "nigridized" or "semitized". The most purely Aryan segment of Europe was the aristocracy. Gobineau's book became a success among the upper classes, which welcomed any idea which could be used to justify their superiority.

For the upper classes of Europe in the late 19th and early 20th centuries, the genius of the concept of anti-semitism was that it accomplished several political objectives at once. The term itself provided a modern, pseudo-scientific gloss for an old-fashioned religious and political tradition. During the middle ages, rulers used theologically inspired dislike of Judaism to explain calamities which medical science could not yet explain. The plague and other epidemics were often blamed on Jews, who were said to have poisoned the wells.[13] After 1850, Europe's upper classes had a more pressing calamity to explain – the growing popular belief in democracy and equality. For the privileged classes, attacking Jews would kill many birds with one stone. Anti-Judaism could be used to justify the principle of inequality since one group at least could be shown to be inherently undeserving. Liberal and socialist parties demanding equality rights could be branded as semitic, especially it they had any Jewish leaders. Liberals and socialists might even be sidetracked into attacking Jews instead of the privileged strata. Finally, the upper classes could use anti-Judaism as a means of creating an emotional bond with the middle and lower strata.

"Anti-semitism" is a relatively recent, pseudo-scientific term conjured up to give a new vigour to the old-fashioned animosity towards Jews. In our book, we speak of anti-Judaism, which describes the subject more simply and more accurately. It is a testimony to its power that anti-Jewish thought in Western civilization is best known by the term which was invoked in the 19th century to justify it.

In the 19th and 20th centuries, anti-Judaism found its greatest expression in countries lacking a strong democratic political tradition. Like the upper classes of Europe whose interests they often represented, Europe's dictatorships were attracted to anti-Judaism as a versatile political weapon.[14] Anti-Judaism could be used to sidetrack criticism of a regime or to cause fear and hysteria in the general population.

Both the Nazi regime and the Soviet regime employed anti-Judaism to deflect criticism away from themselves and to arouse a sense of panic and anxiety which could be used for political purposes. In the end, the German regime went the full length of organizing and carrying out a program of liquidation. Under Stalin, Moscow almost went as far.

In Russia, the political use of anti-Judaism peaked at the end of the Czarist regime, went into abeyance under V.I. Lenin, and then returned under Joseph Stalin during the 1930's. By creating a widespread hysteria about Jews, Stalin struck fear in the hearts of both Jewish and non-Jewish subordinates. Stalin's non-Jewish officials worried that something they said, did, or thought might offend the party secretary, be labelled as Jewish, and lead to their demise. During World War II, Stalin ordered the extermination of the Tatars and other small nationalities occupying the Crimean peninsula, alleging that they were fifth columnists plotting with capitalist armies poised to invade Russia. After the war, Stalin charged Russian Jews with seeking to establish a "bourgeois-zionist" republic in the same area, for the same treacherous purpose. He also accused Jewish physicians of plotting with the U.S. Central Intelligence Agency to poison patriotic Russians by pharmaceutical means. "Murderers in white gowns," he called them. Shortly before his death, Stalin undertook plans for the wholesale relocation and presumably liquidation of the Soviet Jewish population.

Soviet Communist Party Secretary Nikita Khrushchev and Stalin's other successors have had more traditional and modest goals, to use anti-Judaism in order to manage their political opposition. Ukrainians were told that their misfortunes were not the fault of the Kremlin or party but of Jews undermining the system.[15] Poles were told to blame the country's agricultural shortfalls on Rabbis, who allegedly existed in large numbers and sequestered meat. In order to create a gulf between Lech Walensa's Solidarity free trade union movement and the Polish Catholic sub-culture which nurtured it, the Soviet and Polish secret police disseminated broadsheets claiming that Solidarity's leaders were actually Jewish.

Both the Soviet and German Nazi regime employed anti-Judaism as an instrument of foreign policy, especially in the oil-rich middle east. The themes and content of the *Protocols of the Elders of Zion* migrated to the Arab world during the 1930's as a result of German propaganda efforts. The pamphlet itself was widely distributed. Nazi agents provocateurs encouraged Arabs to believe in the existence of a world-wide Jewish conspiracy involving Winston Churchill, Franklin Delano Roosevelt, and the Rockefeller family, all of whom were allegedly Jewish. The idea that the Rockefellers, who are Baptist, are central to an international Jewish conspiracy appeared later in Soviet anti-Jewish propaganda. The middle east was receptive to these ideas for a multitude of reasons. Some of these factors were the rise of Arab nationalism, Islamic revivalism, anti-British and anti-French feelings engendered by the colonial experience, and a sense of outrage that a Jewish and hence non-Moslem state could be created in the midst of the Arab, Moslem civilization.

After World War II, many Nazi agents acquired positions in the propaganda and secret police services of the Syrian, Egyptian, and other Arab governments. Saudi Arabia and its neighbours became major centres for the multilingual publication and dissemination of the *Protocols*. During his trial, Ernst Zundel revealed that he had published *The West, War, and Islam* in the hope of securing financial assistance from like-minded people in the middle east. Zundel was not apparently very successful at acquiring financial support in that region of the world. But, Arab governments did undertake their own efforts to disseminate anti-Jewish views in Canada. In 1985, copies of the *Protocols of the Elders of Zion* were available for sale at 50 cents per copy at nine Canadian campuses thanks to subsidies from middle eastern governments.

The Trial

As seen through the lens of media coverage of the courtroom drama, Ernst Zundel held the lead role. The spotlight focussed on his sworn testimony, his comments to the press, and on his dramatic entrances to and exits from the court. Major supporting roles were given to the solicitors for the defence and for the Crown. Bit parts went to the witnesses for the defence and for the prosecution.

Zundel insisted that he was a fervent pacifist with not an iota of ill-will or hatred towards anyone. He started out, he said, with no views about Jews and certainly no anti-Jewish prejudice. Not all Jews are necessarily bad, in his view. He was interested only in a careful, dispassionate consideration of the facts. The facts he described were vile. Zundel claimed that his extensive research demonstrated that the Holocaust had never taken place, that six million Jews had never died. Jews fabricated the death and torture of their co-religionists in order to acquire political and financial advantage. By persuading people that European Jews had been exterminated, Israel was able to secure Western sympathies while individual Jews were able to extort reparations from the West German government.

Zundel used the services of friendly witnesses from his international network to strengthen the impression that his understanding of European history derived from a consideration of evidence. Zundel's witnesses discussed whether or not gas chambers existed, whether camp inmates were happy, and whether the inmates enjoyed swimming and ballroom dances. The defence witnesses' portrayal of the facts was readily conveyed by the media. "No gas chambers in Nazi Germany, expert witness testifies" was one headline in Toronto's *Globe and Mail*. "Women happy at Auschwitz, trial told" was another *Globe* heading; the subheading was "Guards respectful, ex-soldier says." At the Toronto *Sun*, a headline declared "Auschwitz called fake" with the subheading "Nazi camp had 'pool, ballroom'." Zundel and his solicitor sought to leave the impression that the defence was merely offering another possible scholarly interpretation of the Hitler era. "Lawyer challenges crematoria theory" was one of the *Globe's* headings.

The defence examined the extermination process in macabre detail. Can the chemical zyklon-B (i.e. cyanide) kill people? Could the Auschwitz chambers have really gassed 2000-3000 persons at a time? Would this volume of activity have taken as much as three and a half weeks? What was the colour of the smoke emerging from the camp smokestacks? Do corpses actually smell when incinerated? Were the lampshades truly made of human skin? Did the inmates of Auschwitz hold ballroom dances? Did the camps have fences to prevent the inmates from escaping or were the fences erected to stop outsiders from joining their privileged existence? These were some of the ostensibly objective, scientific questions which Zundel and his supporters claimed to be interested in.

Like ghost stories, Zundel's words elicited media interest by virtue of their sheer ghoulishness. Even when discussing questions which by themselves were not macabre, Zundel and his supporters managed to use imagery of death and domination. Speaking of his native West Germany, Zundel said that the democratic system created after World War II was run by quizzlings and apologists populating a "political cemetery." Zundel wanted to free "Aryans" (i.e. white Christians) from "the shackles of lies and brain manipulation" caused by a conspiracy of Communists, fellow-travellers, Freemasons, and Zionists in the mass media. Jews controled the world through their alleged control of such newspapers as the *Washington Post* and through their alleged control of the Masonic lodges. As evidence that Masonic lodges manipulated the United States, Zundel pointed to alleged masonic symbols on the American dollar bill and to George Washington's alleged membership in a lodge. Zundel feared that white people – Aryans – would remain forever "mental slaves" unless they turned to him for help. One of his supporters, a community college teacher from Alberta, told the court that those in his province who dared to question the Holocaust were socially "anaesthmatized," meaning presumably that they were ostracized.

One defence witness with a particularly macabre tale was Ditleib Felderer, a convicted hate-mongerer who flew in from his native Sweden to lend assistance. During his period on the witness stand, Felderer told the court about his many pamphlets. One of them, ostensibly written by a little girl, contained sketches of children surrounding the text. It asked Auschwitz museum authorities to explain why they are trying to convince children that their displays are true. A flyer invited readers to send a lock of human or animal hair to the camp museum so that it would have some authentic hair for its displays.

The two solicitors in the trial received considerable media coverage especially during their summations at the end. Zundel's counsel was Douglas Christie, a Victoria, B.C. lawyer. Christie had previously been leader of Western Canada Concept, an unsuccessful separatist party in the Western provinces. Zundel hired Christie after seeing him represent Keegstra at a hearing in October, 1984 in Red Deer, Alberta. When he agreed to represent Zundel, Christie announced that he did so solely because he believed that the case involved an important matter of principle – freedom of speech. During the trial itself, the defence counsel alternated between declaring that his client had a right to express his opinion and declaring that his client's opinion was in fact the right one to express.

The Crown attorney was a careful, competent solicitor named Peter Griffiths, who received far less media coverage than the more theatrical Christie. For Christie, the Zundel case was all consuming. Griffiths had a wide range of other pressing obligations in his role as a Crown prosecutor. From the outset, Griffiths was keenly aware of the limited time he could devote to the case, of his limited budgetary resources, and of his limited familiarity with hate propaganda and the Holocaust. He became increasingly concerned that an acquittal by a Canadian court might invigorate the international hate network. The Crown attorney spent many evenings and nights reading scholarly works and government documents on the Holocaust to the point where his detailed knowledge amazed many well informed spectators in the courtroom. He also made careful use of expert advice whenever he could secure it. During the preparations leading up to the trial and during the trial itself, Griffiths sought and received advice from many Jewish and non-Jewish groups and individuals. Within days of being assigned the case, Griffiths began receiving assistance from the B'nai Brith League for Human Rights with respect to identifying witnesses and evaluating evidence.

The trial stretched out over a seven week period. In his concluding remarks to the jury, the Crown attorney called the defendant a dangerous Nazi sympathizer whose innate shrewdness distinguished him from the "band of crazies, misfits and frustrated men" who call themselves Holocaust revisionists. "This man is not only clever, he's dangerous," said Peter Griffiths. "Beneath the dimples, I suggest, is a ruthless and determined man." "What is the major stumbling block to the rehabilitation of the Nazis?" he asked the jury. "I'd suggest it is the Holocaust. So long as the greatest inhumanity man has ever done to man exists as a historically accepted fact in the minds of men, the Nazis can never be rehabilitated. He must get rid of it. So he published a pamphlet replete with lies."

Defence counsel Douglas Christie spoke about the principles of freedom of speech and freedom of belief. Advancing an argument which he would later use to defend James Keegstra, Christie insisted that the right to minority opinions was at stake. "What are we – lobotomized idiots that we can only accept the viewpoint of the majority? . . . Do we have to learn the same lessons all over again every generation? Do we never entrench the right to differ?" Zundel, according to his counsel, was another Galileo, who dared to utter the heresy that the world was round. "For the sake of freedom, I ask you never to forget what is at stake here. The accused stands in the place of anyone who desire to speak their mind. Even if you don't agree with him, you must take it as a sacred responsibility not to allow the suppression of someone else's honest opinion." The interpretation of history is necessarily controversial. According to the lawyer for the defence, it is not for the courts to decide which interpretation is correct and which is false. A guilty verdict would be frighteningly destructive of the democratic process. A guilty verdict would leave dissidents with a narrow choice between silence and violence.

Concluding his address to the jury, defence council Christie insisted that his client was expressing not only an honest opinion but a correct one as well.

The arguments presented in Zundel's booklets were well founded. How could a group of people as numerous as the population of Toronto have been killed at Auschwitz without there being, he said, direct evidence? The lawyer for the defence called upon Jews to accept disagreement. "Stop seeing Nazis every time there is a criticism of Judaism." Christie called upon Jews to accept that the Holocaust did not happen as they think it did. Christie jolted the packed courtroom when his voice rose to a crescendo. "There are powers in this land that don't want you to know the truth about it," he roared.

Crown counsel Peter Griffiths insisted that freedom of speech was not at issue in the trial. Democratic societies encourage freedom of speech, but they cannot permit absolute freedom. "Absolute freedom is another way of talking about tyranny. If I have absolute freedom to do anything I please then I can shoot you, rob you or cheat you. That is not the way to run society. My freedom is your slavery." The prosecutor's argument about freedom's not being an issue was pointedly endorsed by the presiding judge. In his charge to the jury, District Court Judge Hugh Locke stated that the Criminal Code does not prohibit "back-fence gossip" or legitimate debate. But, declared the Judge, all societies need certain restrictions on freedom of speech.

Crown lawyer Griffiths argued that immense harm was done by a single pamphlet, *Did Six Million Really Die?* "Anyone reading this article and believing it to be true couldn't help but loathe Jews. You would see all Jews as world-destroyers bent on chaos." How could any Jew who survived the Holocaust or whose relatives perished greet a booklet suggesting that it never happened? Or, an article that said the Jews of the world are trading on a mythical event to gain war reparations? "Such an article spits on the memory of their loved ones and denies them the dignity of their grief. The memory of those millions demands that the truth of this era forever prevail." Zundel himself was no colourful eccentric or harmless crank but a racist, "a racist who is a determined defamer of the Jewish people."

The implications of the trial are universal, concluded prosecutor Griffiths. "This isn't a case involving just Jews and Germans. It involves all of us." Publications which deny that the Holocaust ever took place must be confronted to make sure that humans "never go down that terrible road again." "Today it's the Jews who are slandered. Tomorrow – the Catholics, the blacks, or me."

Debating the Advisability of Prosecuting Zundel

If one may judge by newspaper commentaries and letters-to-the-editor, the seven week trial engendered a great deal of concern among journalists, professors, and lawyers, especially in English Canada. Many opinion-makers wrote as if they found themselves in a catch-22 situation. On the one hand, they felt that Zundel did not deserve the respect from the law which he received and the large public expenditure entailed in a full-fledged trial. On the other hand, they felt uncomfortable at the precedent for freedom of speech which might be established should he be convicted. Some opinion-makers were concerned that the law was being used to rectify the mistakes of education. If Canadians had learned the facts of the Holocaust in school, it might be less necessary to employ the law to silence the hate-mongerers.

Some opinion-makers were also concerned about the consequences of an unsuccessful prosecution. An acquittal would embolden Nazis. Although an acquittal would likely be reached on the basis of a concern for freedom of speech, hatemongerers would likely misrepresent the court's decision as support for Holocaust denial. In the aftermath of Zundel's conviction, Crown prosecutor Peter Griffiths expressed considerable personal concern about the harm which would result from an acquittal in this or any other hate propaganda case.[16] As Griffiths and others have pointed out, Canadian hate legislation favours the defence. The crown must prove that the accused *knowingly* told harmful untruths or *knowingly* fomented hatred. It is much easier to persuade a jury that an accused told harmful lies or caused hatred than that the accused did so knowingly.

During the first weeks of the trial, so much concern was expressed about the advisability of the prosecution that it almost seemed as if prosecutor Peter Griffiths or the Attorney-General of the Ontario was the villain of the piece rather than the accused. Reporting at the conclusion of the trial, a staff writer for Ottawa's *Citizen* noted that most lawyers and experts believed that the case should never have gone to trial.[17] The Director of Communications for the League for Human Rights of B'nai Brith was reported by the *Globe and Mail* as acknowledging that many people with whom she had discussed the matter, Jewish and Christian alike, opposed the prosecution.[18] University of Western Ontario Law Professor Robert Martin declared that "it was profoundly stupid to charge Zundel."[19] He should simply have been deported. Longtime Tory grey eminence Dalton Camp said that it had been a grave mistake. "In the zealous attempt to prosecute a fool for his beliefs we make fools of ourselves."[20]

Alan Borovoy, general counsel to the Canadian Civil Liberties Association, said flatly that "acquitted or convicted, it was a most unwise prosecution."[21] He worried that the trial would have a chilling effect on legitimate historical discussions. Borovoy conceded that Zundel represented a clear case where almost everyone could agree with respect to the evil motives of the accused. However, he was concerned about more ambiguous cases in the future. He was also concerned about providing Zundel with a platform. The trial gave "legitimacy . . . to a very illegitimate organization. Legitimacy has been conferred on garbage." Borovoy observed that the word "theory was now widely used to describe crematoria. Understood as a fact 40 years ago, the existence of crematoria now becomes a theory." The death camps are now portrayed as Jewish country clubs, all "at public expense."

Fear that the trial would gain publicity for the Nazis and confer legitimacy on them was the single most widespread reason for being against the trial. Former national secretary of the New Democratic Party Gerald Caplan opposed the prosecution because he felt that Zundel and his ilk should be "left under the boulders where they belong."[22] Prosecution was "a terrible, terrible blunder." Toronto's scholar-rabbi-journalist, Gunther Plaut, opposed the prosecution for much the same reason. He was perturbed that Zundel had been afforded the legitimacy of a hearing in court. "I think it was an error, regardless of how it comes out. Even if the jury convicts, I'm not happy. The pseudo-legitimacy they have been given is very harmful."[23]

After the jury reached its verdict, *Toronto Star* columnist Frank Jones described at length why the trial would do harm. The guilty verdict was better than a not guilt verdict, but it was "no triumph." The damage was done. *"Quietly, like a thief in the night, the insidious ideas of Zundel and his gang have sneaked their way into the consciousness of the young who may not know better and into the minds of some of their elders grasping for any straw to justify their prejudices."* According to columnist Jones, the trial provided an unsurpassed grandstand. "It was an opportunity to spread his lies far and wide. And so we had first the revolting spectacle of Holocaust survivors being grilled and belittled in the witness box. And then, for three weeks, we were treated to a sort of academic debate in which bogus experts were accorded respect, just like learned professors earnestly debating the Punic wars of ancient Greece."[24]

The ideal that the trial gained exposure for Nazism was accepted as axiomatic among both supporters and opponents of bringing the case to trial. Sabina Citron and other Rememberance Association activists did not dispute the view that the trial would and did provide Zundel with immense publicity. They believed that Zundel had already done serious harm. In their view, leaving the propaganda unchallenged for years enabled it to become increasingly inflammatory.[25] "Everyone knows what unchecked hate propaganda can lead to." Assuming that it would eventually become necessary to confront the Holocaust denial propagandists at some time in some fashion, it was better to hold a trial early while some Holocaust survivors were still able to testify. Supporters of the prosecution also took the view that it was better to confront the revisionists before they became too numerous.

Most proponents as well as opponents of prosecution talked about the public impact of the trial as if the public consisted of an indistinguishable mass of likeminded people. One important exception was David Humphrey, the Toronto lawyer who acted for the Rememberance Association. He conceded that the trial gave free publicity to the defendant. But, he distinguished between the trial's impact on extremists and on reasonable people. "Of course, he's won," said lawyer Humphrey of Zundel. "If he gets a year in jail, he's won. He got international press. His name is a household word. He has won to the subculture who thinks he has won, but to right-thinking people, he's lost."[26] Alan Shefman of the League for Human Rights of B'nai Brith also expressed doubt that Zundel was quite as clever as many people thought he was. Shefman opined that Zundel had won "one million dollars of notoriety."[27]

Perhaps the most thoughtful commentary on the whole episode was by Robert Fulford, editor of Canada's pre-eminent journal of arts and letters. In an artice in *Saturday Night,* Fulford wrote that liberal democracies have enormous difficulty dealing with genuine evil.[28] We do not know how to react and therefore become confused. If our legal system ignores our hate mongerers, the hate mongerers are given implicit legitimacy. But, if they are brought to trial, they must be given a respectful hearing as if they were motivated by high principles, which they are not.

A journalist himself, Fulford expressed the view that the practice of journalism is a vital aspect of the problem, as important as the legal system. Fulford agreed with Zundel's own assessment that the trial had generated "one million dollars of free publicity." According to Fulford, the enormous uncritical publicity which Zundel received from the trial was a direct result of the rigid conventions of journalism, which hold that the press should report only what happens in public. Extremists are able to gain exposure for repeated lies because their lies are not evaluated for their truthfulness. As journalism is practiced, the task of the reporter is to convey what a newsworthy person has said in public and not to transmit information which might help evaluate the truthfulness of what is said.

Fulford compared the role of journalism in the rise of U.S. Senator Joseph McCarthy, the leader of the anti-Communist witch-hunt in the 1950's, with the role of journalism in legitimating Zundel's Holocaust fabrications. Joseph McCarthy repeatedly proclaimed that he had long lists of crypto-Communists in the highest echelons of the United States government. McCarthy had no such names. He was bluffing. But, uncritical media reports on his speeches helped to create a mood of national paranoia. The Canadian press fulfilled much the same role during the Zundel trial, said Fulford, because it reported both sides as if each were credible. Thus, when France's convicted hate mongerer, Rober Faurisson, testified, the *Globe and Mail's* headline was "No gas chambers in Nazi Germany, expert says." Fulford did not go sofar as to suggest that the Canadian media created a climate of Holocaust denial akin to the anti-Communist hysteria generated by Joseph McCarthy in the 1950's. But, Fulford did say that whatever inroads were made by Zundel among the Canadian public were a result of the rigid conventions of the media.

Many commentators on the trial discussed the trial's impact on public attitudes towards Jews or Nazis. Few people speculated about the trial's impact on public attitudes towards Germans or German Canadians. A notable and distinguished exception was Peter Hessel, an author and German-born public servant working for the Canadian government.[29] Hessel expressed no sympathy for Zundel. He noted that Zundel's fellow extremists had been sentenced to prison in West Germany. Hessel was profoundly concerned that the trial would succeed in tarring all German Canadians with the same brush. Ashamed of both Zundel and the war crimes, Hessel worried that Zundel's grandstanding would set back the efforts of German Canadians to regain the respect which they had lost as a result of the Holocaust.

The central motivation for our research project was to find out what truly happened in the mind of the Canadian public. Did support for the Nazi perspective grow as a result of the trial and as a result of media coverage of the trial? Did more Canadians become prejudiced against Jews as a result of the affair? How were attitudes towards Germans affected? What specific roles did television and the press have in shaping Canadian attitudes? Were the media as harmful as many people, including journalists, feared? Was it a case of "one million dollars worth of publicity" or "one million dollars worth of notoriety"?

As we thought more and more about our project, it occurred to us that our research findings could have general ramifications for the advisability of holding any hate propaganda trial. Although Jews have been a major target of hatred, in North America they are not the sole target of hate. Native people, Chinese and Japanese Canadians, Canadians of East Indian origin, blacks, Franco-Ontarians, Roman Catholics and other groups have been the target of victimization in various provinces at various times in Canadian history.

As we thought more and more about the project, it occurred to us that the trial's impact on public opinion ought to be examined in a broad context. What kinds of Canadians were traditionally prejudiced against Jews and what kinds were traditionally unprejudiced? Did the trial affect all Canadians in a similar fashion? Or, did some Canadians become more prejudiced while others became less prejudiced? Did the trial affect the attitudes of Canadians towards the Jews of the Holocaust only, or did it also affect attitudes towards Jews as Canadians? These are some of the research questions for which we sought answers.

1 Unless otherwise indicated, all quotes in this chapter are drawn from the *Info-Globe* retrieval service of the *Globe and Mail*.

2 Crown prosecutor Peter Griffiths, address to the University of Ottawa Law Faculty, October, 1985.

3 In 1978, Julius Israeli, a Holocaust survivor and former university professor, began his longterm efforts to bring the force of law against school teacher Malcolm Ross. Ross' book *The Web of Deceit* and his pamphlet *Christianity vs. Judeo-Christianity - the Battle for the Truth* warn against an international communist-Jewish conspiracy. His book *The Real Holocaust, the Attack on Unborn Children and Life Itself* portrays the pro-abortion movement as an international Jewish conspiracy to depopulate white Christian civilization.

4 *Globe and Mail*, February 28th, 1985, p. 1.

5 See "Racial tolerance the winner in Zundel case, " *Toronto Star*, March 2nd, 1985, by Harold Levy, editor of the Criminal Lawyers' Association Newsletter.

6 McGill University Professors Ruth Wisse and Irwin Cotler distinguish between "classical anti-Semitism, which denied the equal rights of Jews as citizens within a free society (and) . . . 'new' anti-Semitism, which denies the equal right of the Jewish people as a lawful sovereignty within the family of nations. "Quebec's Jews: Caught in the Middle," *Commentary* 64 (1977) 3, 58.

7 See Robert Fulford's discussion in *Saturday Night* (June, 1985).

8 Carleton University *Charlatan* (March 14th, 1985), p. 12

9 Carleton University's *Charlatan* (March 14th, 1985), p. 12

10 This brief overview of Carto's network was made possible by information supplied by Alan Shefman of B'nai Brith's League for Human Rights. The climate of opinion encouraged by Carto's publications helped to make possible the growth of the violent neo-Nazi Order or Silent Brotherhood in the United States. By coincidence, during the course of the Zundel trial in Toronto, the U.S. Federal Bureau of Investigation undertook a sweep of Nazis in seven states. The FBI sought a number of fugitives for their role in bank robberies, undertaken to finance their "war" against the U.S. government, which these groups considered to be under Jewish control. The police held the Order responsible for the assassination of Alan Berg. Until his death, Berg was a talk show host in Denver, Colorado, well known for his sympathy for the Black civil rights movement. The Order reportedly murdered one of their own members who was suspected of acting for the FBI. *New York Times*, March 3rd, 1985, p. 20

[11] Norman Cohn, *Warrant for Genocide: the Myth of the Jewish World Conspiracy and the Protocols of the Elders of Zion* (London: Penuin, 1970). See also Alan Davies, "On Religious Myths and their Secular Translation: Some Historical Reflections" in Alan T. Davies, ed., *Anti-Semitism and the Foundations of Christianity* (Toronto: Paulist Press, 1979).

[12] James Parkes, *Anti-Semitism* (Chicago: Quadrangle Books, 1969), chapter IV on "The Protocols of the Elders of Zion."

[13] The poisoning of wells and other medieval anti-Jewish themes persist in the Soviet press today. For example, after the Israeli invasion of Lebanon, Soviet newspapers carried cartoons of Israeli soldiers pouring cannisters marked poison into Lebanese wells.

[14] In his study of the first eight centuries of Christian history, James Parkes also found a pattern whereby repressive measures agains Jews were more apt to be taken by unpopular rulers than by popular ones. See his *The Conflict of the Church and the Synagogue* (Toronto: McClelland and Stewart, 1974), p. 349.

[15] See the intriguing essays in Howard Aster and Peter J. Potichnyj, *Jewish Ukrainian Relations: Two Solitudes* (Oakville: Mosaic Press, 1983).

[16] Address, University of Ottawa Law Faculty, October, 1985. A similar point has frequently been made by David Matas, counsel to the B'nai Brith League for Human Rights.

[17] March 2nd, 1985, p. B1.

[18] This statement appeared in the edition of February 28th, p. 1, but was apparently made several weeks earlier.

[19] *Citizen,* March 2nd, 1985, p. B1.

[20] *Saturday Night,* June, 1985, p. 8.

[21] *Citizen,* March 2nd, 1985, p. B1.

[22] *Saturday Night,* June, 1985, p. 8.

[23] *Globe and Mail,* February 28th, 1985, p. 1.

[24] *Toronto Star,* March 1st, 1985.

[25] *Citizen,* March 2nd, 1985, p. B1.

[26] *Globe and Mail,* February 28th, 1985, p. 1.

[27] "Cross-Country Checkup," CBC radio, March 3rd, 1985.

[28] Peter Hessel, "Herr Zundel, you're in an enemy world," *Citizen,* Weekend Observer, March 9th, 1985.

Chapter 2

Public Awareness of the Trial

The preceding chapter discussed the prevalent view among those who commented on the trial in the media that the trial had a major impact on the public. Fear of a major negative impact on the public mind was a common reason for people to have doubts about the advisability of bringing the accused to trial. Even those who, like Sabina Citron, were most desirous of a trial did not apparently deny the possibility that the trial might influence public opinion or that the accused might use his performance on the witness stand to gain adherents outside the courtroom. For the trial to have had an impact on the minds of Canadians, it had to have been covered generously by television and the press. It was indeed reported generously.

Our analysis of major national and regional newspapers from coast to coast as well as the news services of the English and French television services of the Canadian Broadcasting Corporation showed that the trial did receive an extraordinary level of attention, especially among the English-language media. English Canada's most influential newspaper, the *Globe and Mail,* assigned a reporter to the story. So did the Canadian Press wire-service, the *Toronto Star,* CBC, CTV, the *Washington Post,* the *Boston Globe,* the *Chicago Tribune,* and CBS television. During the key period, January 1st to March 15th, 1985, Toronto's *Globe and Mail* carried a total of 31 stories and 8 pictures. On average, a story on the trial appeared *almost every other day.* An extraordinary six stories appeared on the top of page 1 along with two pictures. On Wednesday, January 16th, the paper headlined its story "One-way rail fares point to slaughter, Zundel is told." The story headline the following day was "Holocaust scholar quoted 'madman,' publishing trial is told." On January 18th, the story was headlined "German prisoners tortured by Americans, trial is told." On Saturday, January 19th, the story headline was "Testimony at Zundel trial draws tears." Readers were spared a Zundel story until the following Wednesday, when the paper began another four days in succession of trial reports.

The *Globe and Mail* might be expected to provide generous coverage of the trial because it took place in the newspaper's home town and because Toronto contains a large Jewish community which might be expected to want to follow the trial. However, this cannot be a satisfactory explanation for the *Globe's* coverage because the trial received intense coverage almost from coast to coast. Three thousand miles away in a city with a very small Jewish community, the *Vancouver Sun* provided approximately the same level of coverage. The *Sun* carried only one front page story as compared to the six front page stories in the *Globe*, but the *Sun* carried 33 stories and 8 pictures as compared to the *Globe's* 31 and 10, respectively. One Vancouver headline was "Human Smoke at Nazi Camp disputed." Another headline was "Camp ordeal described in Holocaust hoax case."

Other regional papers also reported the trial in considerable detail. The *Calgary Herald* carried 29 stories including one on the front page as well as two pictures, one of which was also on the front page. Even the *Evening Standard* of St. John's, Newfoundland, far removed geographically and psychologically from the trial, provided more than trivial coverage. During the January 1st to March 15th, 1985 period, the Newfoundland paper carried a total of 12 stories for an average of about one story for each five printing days. Newspapers in Halifax, Winnipeg, and Saskatoon likewise carried a sufficient volume of reporting for readers to be able to follow the trial.

Those English-speaking Canadians who do not read the daily press could nonetheless follow the trial if they watched television or listened to the radio.[1] The *National* newsprogram of the CBC television English service and the *Journal* public affairs program mated to it provided a total of 30 stories on Zundel and his trial during the period from January 1st to April 28th. During the month of February, the *National* was saturated with Zundel stories. At least one such story appeared each day during the last week of the month. On February 28th, the 10 p.m. *National* devoted more than five minutes to the trial verdict, a substantial amount of time by news standards. The *Journal* followed with a thirty minute review of the entire trial. A regular viewer of CBC news would have enormous difficulty avoiding exposure to information about the trial.

Canadian television broadcasts are able to reach almost every household in the country and Canadians watch a lot of Canadian news. More than 98% of Canadians own at least one television set and almost all TV viewers are able to watch Canadian broadcasts. In the field of television drama, Canadians – especially English-speakers – watch mainly American shows. Canadians are also more apt to watch American than Canadian variety and quiz shows.

But, when it comes to news programs, Canadians tune to Canadian broadcasts. French-Canadians rarely watch American news shows. English Canadians watch Canadian news programs about 90% of the time.[2]

If there was one group of Canadians who might have missed being exposed to a significant amount of reporting on the trial, this group consisted of French-speaking Canadians. *Téléjournal* and *Le Point,* the French language counterparts of the *National* and the *Journal,* carried much less coverage. As the editor-in-chief of Radio Canada television news said to one of the authors, "We didn't give the subject as much coverage as the English network because the issue was not as important for Quebecers."[3] Montreal's respected French language daily, *La Presse,* carried only eight reports on the trial, less than one-third of the coverage provided by the Toronto, Calgary, and Vancouver papers in our study and less coverage even than the Newfoundland paper. Quebec City's *Le Soleil* contained still less information. The newspaper in the provincial capital carried but one back page story during the entire period in question. The different responses to the trial of the English and French media are an important fact, a fact to which we will return in later chapters.

In order to study the impact of the trial on the Canadian public, we designed and commissioned a national survey of adult Canadians. The survey was conducted in mid-March, after the defendant had been convicted but before he received his sentence of 15 months in prison and a two year prohibition on discussing the Holocaust. A random sample of 1054 Canadians at least 18 years old was interviewed in person. When proper procedures are followed in selecting respondents to be interviewed and when a questionnaire is properly constructed, the attitudes and opinions revealed by a sample of one thousand Canadians can be treated with considerable confidence as reflecting the attitudes and opinions of all Canadians.

As in the case of most national and international events, Ernst Zundel's trial in a Toronto courtroom could only have become known to the average Canadian through the mass media. Our questionnaire asked respondents to reveal the degree to which they used television and newspapers to follow the news.[4] Interviewees were asked how often during the preceding seven days they had watched news broadcasts on television and how often they had read news reports in the newspaper. Their responses show that Canadians are heavy news addicts. More than three-quarters of the sample said that they watched television news at least three times a week. Over half reported that they did not miss a single day. Generally, fewer people read the news columns of their daily paper than watched the nightly news. Yet, more than one third (37%) read the news columns every single day while almost two-thirds (62%) read them at least three days a week.

Chapter 1 discussed the prevalent opposition to Zundel's prosecution among Canadians who expressed a view on this matter because they feared that the trial would have a substantial, negative impact on public attitudes towards Jews. To this point in our analysis, it looks as if the prophets of doom were right. The media not only granted enormous coverage but Canadians are gluttons for news. Yet, to show that the media provided enormous coverage and that people watch television news and read papers does not necessarily demonstrate that people absorb the information to which they are exposed. Scholars of communication have shown that people do not absorb or remember everything that they watch or read. Viewers or readers may ignore information if it carries no immediate relevance to their daily lives, if the information is not easily understood, or if the information is about an event which disturbs them and is beyond their control.[5]

To find out if Canadians were indeed aware of the trial, we asked respondents the following simple question: *"The media have talked a lot about a recent court trial in Toronto of Ernst Zundel. Do you happen to know what Ernst Zundel was convicted of?"* The question was of the type known as "open-ended." Interviewers did not offer respondents a choice among several possible answers. Respondents were expected, and if necessary, invited to answer the question in their own words. For purposes of our analysis we used the respondent's knowledge of why Zundel was convicted as a measure of his or her awareness or knowledge of the trial. In describing, below, those respondents who could state correctly why Zundel was charged, we use the adjectives aware, informed, and knowledgeable interchangeably.

Interviewers were instructed to code responses as either correct or incorrect. Virtually any plausible answer was to be recorded as correct. A response was coded as correct if a respondent said that Zundel had been convicted of "causing harm to racial or social harmony," "distributing hate literature," "claiming the Holocaust was a hoax," "anti-semitic literature," or "promoting hatred against Jews." If the interviewer believed the answer to be incorrect, the answer was written down word-for-word and double-checked to insure that no part of the answer could be considered correct. Everything was done to make it possible for respondents to answer the question correctly. Furthermore, the survey was conducted, readers may recall, at a high point in the trial, after the conviction and before the sentencing.

A Note to Readers on Understanding Statistics in this Book

Our book has been written for three types of readers: those who feel uncomfortable reading statistics, those people who like to follow basic quantitative patterns, and those who like to read detailed statistical information. Those readers who do not like to read statistical figures or tables can safely skip over all figures and tables in the book. The written text explains everything. Those people who like to follow basic quantitative patterns but no more are welcome to scan the bar and pie diagrams in the *figures*. If confused by any figure, readers can turn to the bottom of the figure for a brief explanation under the heading "interpretation." Readers who love statistics are welcome to read the detailed statistical tables.

If Zundel had succeeded in carrying his message to the country, a large majority of Canadians ought to have been able to answer the question correctly. To have been influenced by the trial in a significant way, they ought to have had at least a vague idea of why the defendant was charged. Yet, our *opinion data showed that only half of Canadians could answer the question correctly.* Half either admitted that they did not know or provided a wrong answer (see fig. 2.1).[6] This finding stands in sharp contrast with the claim that prosecuting Zundel gave him publicity and recognition. The defendant himself proclaimed that he had received "one million dollars of publicity" at an impromptu press conference held after the jury's verdict was announced.

Fig 2.1
Knowing Why Zundel Was Convicted

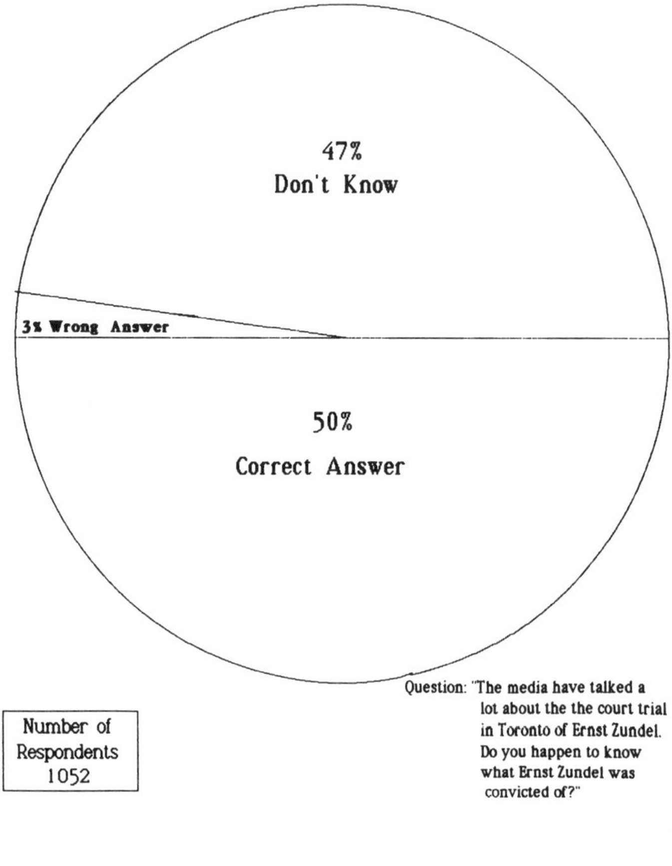

Curious as to why only half of Canadians knew enough about the trial to explain why the defendant was charged and convicted, we looked at the characteristics of those people who knew and those who did not. First, we compared the demographic characteristics of the two groups, for example where they lived and what language they spoke. We then looked at the relig ious and other beliefs of those who did and those who did not know.

Demographic Characteristics

We explored the degree of awareness of the trial among Canadians using a large number of demographic characteristics. We compared the provinces inhabited by our respondents to see whether people in some provinces were more aware of the trial than people in other provinces. We compared our respondents' awareness of the trial according to the size of the community in which they lived and according to whether their community was essentially urban or rural. We compared respondents with respect to their age, gender, personal income, language, extent of education, type of job or occupation, and religious affiliation. Canadians, we found, were by no means homogeneous in their awareness of the trial. They varied in their awareness according to each one of these demographic characteristics (see table 2.1).

Some of the demographic differences were modest in size as well as obvious and predictable. For example, the residents of urban areas were better informed than non-urban dwellers. Among city people, 52% knew why Zundel was convicted as compared to only 45% among the farming population and only 43% among rural dwellers who do not earn their living from agriculture. Young people were somewhat less informed than older people. The best informed were those aged 35 to 44. In this group, as many as 55% knew why Zundel was convicted. A majority of respondents aged 45-59 and over 60 years old also knew. Among respondents in the 25-34 and under-25 age groups, only 47% and 39%, respectively, knew the correct answer.

The occupation, income, and education of respondents also had predictable relationships to their awareness of the trial. People in prestigious occupations tended to be better informed than those in low status positions. For example, 70% of professionals understood why Zundel was charged as compared to 49% of skilled labourers and 47% of unskilled labourers. Interestingly, respondents who said that they were in "sales" were somewhat more likely to be informed than those who indicated that they were business executives (60% vs. 53%). Perhaps people in sales have more free time to follow the news and have more reason to follow the news as well. For sales people, discussing the events of the day can be a way of establishing a rapport with customers.

Like respondents in prestigious occupations, respondents with high personal incomes were well informed. Among respondents with annual incomes of less than $10,000, just less than two-fifths (39%) could explain the nature of Zundel's conviction. The proportion who were aware of the trial rose to 47% among those with incomes in the $20,000-29,999 range and to 64% among those earning more than $40,000.

The occupation and income of respondents were less important factors contributing to their awareness than their education. People who occupy prestigious positions and/or earn high incomes are generally well educated. It makes sense to attribute at least part of the greater knowledge among professionals and high income earners to their greater level of education. Indeed, education is a stronger statistical predictor of awareness of the trial than either income or occupation. Among income and occupation groupings, the best informed groups were less than twice as likely to be aware of the trial than the least informed groups. But, among educational groupings, the best informed group was almost three times as likely to know as the least informed group. Among the most poorly educated respondents – those with some primary education – only one-fourth could explain why Zundel was charged. More than half of high school graduates knew the answer. Among respondents exposed to post-graduate studies at university, the proportion rose to almost three-quarters.

Table 2:1
Awareness of the Zundel Trial Among Demographic Groups

Region	**% Yes**	**% No***	**Total**
Newfoundland	29	71	100 (31)
Nova Scotia	50	50	100 (30)
New Brunswick	28	73	100 (40)
Quebec	29	71	100 (271)
Ontario	61	39	100 (369)
Manitoba	48	53	100 (40)
Saskatchewan	66	34	100 (50)
Alberta	57	44	100 (99)
British Columbia	66	34	100 (122)

	% Yes	% No*	Total
Area			
Urban	52	48	100 (808)
Rural	43	57	100 (193)
Farm	45	55	100 (57)
Language			
English	60	40	100 (634)
French	26	74	100 (285)
Other	58	42	100 (128)
Age			
Under 25	39	61	100 (153)
25-34	47	53	100 (244)
35-44	55	45	100 (199)
45-59	54	44	100 (218)
60 and over	51	49	100 (211)
Sex			
Male	56	44	100 (529)
Female	44	56	100 (523)
Income			
Under 10,000	39	61	100 (112)
10,000-14,999	45	55	100 (101)
15,000-19,999	44	56	100 (82)
20,000-29,999	47	53	100 (182)
30,000-39,999	57	44	100 (168)
40,000 and over	64	36	100 (193)
Education			
Completed elementary	37	63	100 (394)
Completed high school	55	45	100 (516)
Graduated university	68	32	100 (138)
Occupation**			
Professional	70	30	100 (87)
Business Executive	53	47	100 (93)

Sales	60	40	100 (45)
Clerical	51	50	100 (99)
Skilled Labour	49	51	100 (140)
Unskilled Labour	47	53	100 (91)
Unemployed	46	54	100 (37)
Housewife	58	42	100 (250)
Student	49	51	100 (65)
Religious Affiliation			
Anglican	54	56	100 (113)
United Church	60	41	100 (158)
Baptist	78	28	100 (23)
Lutheran	72	28	100 (36)
Presbyterian	54	46	100 (24)
Other Protestant	53	47	100 (75
Roman Catholic	38	62	100 (427)
English RC's	61	39	100 (135)
French RC's	24	76	100 (247)

*Not informed is either "don't know" or wrong answer.
**See appendix C for constructing occupational categories.

N.B. In this and subsequent tables, totals may add up to more than 100% as a result of rounding errors.

Awareness of the Trial among Demographic Groups

That the most educated Canadians are three times more likely to be aware of the Zundel trial than the least educated is a fact of considerable importance. It shows that Canadians are not blank tablets for the media to leave their messages upon. The education which Canadians receive affects both their motivation and their ability to learn about the world around them. Higher education provides young adults with a foundation of knowledge to which they can integrate new facts. Higher education also trains people in techniques for assimilating unanticipated information in the future.

The enormous impact of education on awareness of the trial may help to explain why the journalists and experts exaggerated the influence of the trial. People like *Saturday Night* editor Robert Fulford and civil liberties spokesman Alan Borovoy are not only highly educated but they have a lifetime commitment to intellectual pursuit. Their fears that many people would hear Zundel's message and hence be susceptible to it stems logically from their own worlds, in which almost everyone they know is likely informed about Ernst Zundel and his colleagues.

Gender was a factor in the degree of awareness of the trial among Canadians. In the era of the feminist movement and the migration of women from creche to workplace, it came as a surprise that women were less aware of the trial than men(44% vs. 56%). In the past, women were customarily less informed about public affairs since the world outside the home was widely considered the preserve of men. The fact that women are less aware of the trial may be interpreted as an accidental result of the fact that women, especially older women, are less educated than men.

To explore this possible interpretation, we compared the levels of awareness among men and women of identical levels of education. The greater awareness among men did not disappear. On the contrary, the gap between men and women increased at higher levels of education. Among respondents with only public school education, 42% of males were aware of the trial as compared to 32% of females. Among those with secondary school education, the rates of awareness were 61% among men and 50% among women. Among university graduates, the rates were 77% for males and 56% for females.

It is beyond the mandate of this book to explain these male female differences, but some speculation may be forgiven. One possible explanation is that women continue to see politics and public affairs as mainly a masculine domain. Another possibility is that women are less informed about the trial because the trial entails discussions of war and violence. Women may be less interested in war than men and less militaristic.

To this point, we have examined demographic characteristics which are commonly associated with knowledge of public affairs. Among the industrial democracies of the world, there is a general tendency for the best informed citizens to be highly educated, well paid, high status urban males in their middle years. Nothing reported so far was surprising except perhaps for the sharp difference among highly and poorly educated people and for the persistent difference between men and women.

We did find some surprising results. We compared the levels of awareness of the trial among the provinces.[7] The differences were extraordinary by any yardstick. The provinces broke down into three categories with respect to awareness of the trial: British Columbia, Saskatchewan and Ontario at the high end *vs.* Quebec, Newfoundland and New Brunswick at the low end *vs.* Manitoba, Nova Scotia, and Alberta in between. Two-thirds of respondents in British Columbia and Saskatchewan knew why Zundel was charged as compared to only 28% in New Brunswick and 29% in Quebec and Newfoundland.

The inter-provincial differences in awareness were greater than differences associated with age, gender, income, occupation, and a host of other factors. Only education was a stronger predictor of knowledge of the trial, and only barely so. The journalists and experts talked about Canadians as if they were a single homogenous people. Yet, in terms of their awareness of this all important trial, Canadians act as if they belong to two or perhaps even three distinct nations.

The low awareness of the trial in Quebec and New Brunswick was closely related to language. One obvious factor is that these two provinces contain large French-speaking populations. Another factor is that the French press gave little coverage to the event. Our poll showed that English Canadians were almost two-and-a-half times more likely to be aware of the trial than French Canadians (60% vs. 26%). Taken as a whole, Roman Catholics were less informed than other denominations (see table 2.1). But, the difference between English and French Catholics was much greater than the difference between Catholics and Protestants. As many as 61% of English Catholics were aware of the trial as compared to only 24% of French Catholics. Among the Protestant groups, the best informed were the Lutherans (72%) and the Baptists (78%).

The low levels of awareness in Eastern Canada (Nova Scotia excepted) and among francophones were real cultural differences which cannot readily be attributed to accidental factors such as education. Educated francophones were much less likely to be aware of the trial than educated anglophones. The high level of information among members of the Lutheran and especially Baptist churches were also real differences since neither group was especially well educated. These were important differences in awareness which will reappear through this text as we seek to unravel the puzzle of how the trial impacted upon public opinion.

Overall, the data suggest that awareness of the trial was highest among the following groups of people:

* university graduates
* high income earners
* English Canadians
* residents of British Columbia, Saskatchewan, and Ontario
* Baptists and Lutherans

* professionals
* urban dwellers
* people in their middle years

Awareness of the trial was lowest among:

* people with only primary schooling
* residents of New Brunswick, Quebec, and Newfoundland
* low income earners
* French Canadians
* Roman Catholics
* unemployed
* women
* rural dwellers
* young people

At this point, we conclude our exploration of how differences in awareness of the trial could be explained by standard demographic characteristics such as language and religion. We now turn to an examination of religious and political beliefs. Did the religious beliefs held by people affect their awareness of the trial?

Religious Beliefs

From the end of World War II to the present day, Western scholars have been so perplexed and troubled by Nazism and the Holocaust that they have devoted considerable energies to explain both the rise of Hitler and the presence of anti-Judaism. Canadian scholars have contributed two widely acclaimed books in the area. One book explained how Hitler managed to get elected in Germany. Another showed the great lengths to which Canada's Mackenzie King government went to prevent European Jews from finding refuge from the Holocaust in Canada.[8] But, Canadian scholars have not conducted systematic research into how the Canadian public has felt about Jews and why.[9]

The task of studying public opinion has been embraced enthusiastically by American scholars, particularly during the 1960's. Based at the Survey Research Center at the University of California at Berkley, American sociologists conducted several in depth national and regional polls of American attitudes in order to discover the sources of anti-Jewish hate. They found that people hostile to Jews tended to be ethnocentric or generally hostile to blacks, Asians, and other ethnic outgroups. Like Archie Bunker of television fame, ethnocentric Americans tend to be poorly educated and uninformed. In the particular case of anti-Judaism, the American scholars also found theological roots to prejudice.

The classic study of the question, entitled *Christian Beliefs and Anti-Semitism*[10], found abundant evidence among Americans in the 1960's that those who hated Jews tended to be those devout Christians who lacked a sense of religious tolerance. From national and regional surveys, sociologists Glock and Stark found that theologically committed Christians tended to believe that only Christians are favoured by God, that the ancient Jews were responsible for killing Jesus, and that modern Jews are cursed by God as a result. The perception that Jews are cursed by God led to unfavourable secular views of Jews, for example to the view that Jews cheat. Not all theologically committed Christians were found to be hostile to Jews. The exceptions were those Christians whose sense of religious tolerance led them to favour freedom for non-Christian groups as a whole.

For reasons of economy, we chose not to use every survey question used by the American scholars in their in depth study of Christian theological belief and anti-Judaism. Instead, we focussed on two facets – a commitment to Christian theological belief and a sense of tolerance towards non-Christian religious minorities. We measured the Christian theological commitment of our respondents by their answers to the question, *"Do you think that it is necessary for a person to believe in Jesus Christ to go to heaven?"* Respondents could say that this statement was completely true, probably true, probably not true, or definitely not true. A sense of religious tolerance or religious libertarianism was measured by whether respondents agreed or disagreed with the statement, *"Missionaries from Christian religions should not have the same right to spread their teachings as Christian missionaries."*

It might be revealing to know the degree of awareness of the trial among narrow Christian believers and among religiously intolerant Christians. The degree of awareness among narrow and among intolerant Christians might provide a hint as to how the trial affected Canadians' attitudes towards Jews. If narrow-minded or intolerant Christians were more aware of the trial than their broadminded and tolerant co-religionists, this might be a clue that the trial had encouraged anti-Jewish feeling.

Figs. 2.2 and 2.3 show the opposite pattern. *Narrowminded, intolerant Christians were less aware of the trial than their broadminded, tolerant co-religionists.* The fact that those Canadians who were potentially most receptive to Zundel's message were less aware of the trial suggest that Zundel may have failed in disseminating his viewpoint. Anyone whose task is persuasion must begin by targetting his appeal to those sectors of society most persuadable. The proportion aware of the trial was only 46% among people who believe that heaven is for Christians only. The proportion aware of the trial was as high as 61% among people who think that heaven can accommodate non-Christians as well. The same pattern applies in the case of attitudes towards the rights of non-Christian missionaries. Canadians who favoured equal rights for non-Christian missionaries were slightly more apt to know about the trial than those who opposed equal rights (55% vs. 43%).

Fig 2.2
Knowledge of the Trial and Religious Belief

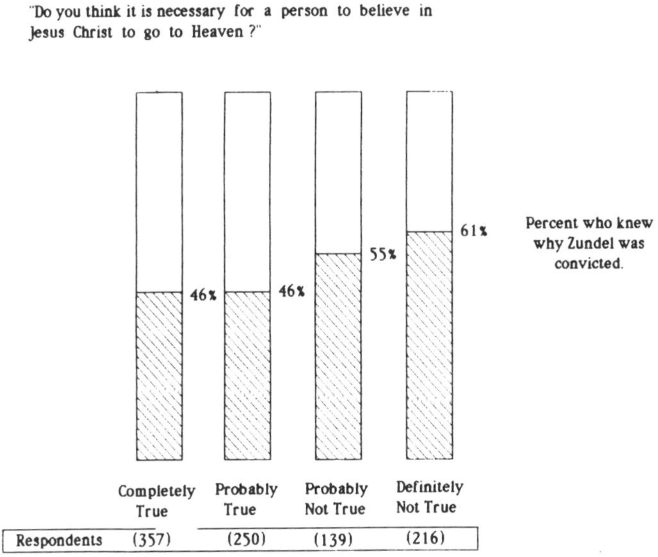

Interpretation: Partisan Christian believers were slightly less knowledgeable of the trial.

Fig 2.3
Knowledge of the Trial
and Religious Tolerance

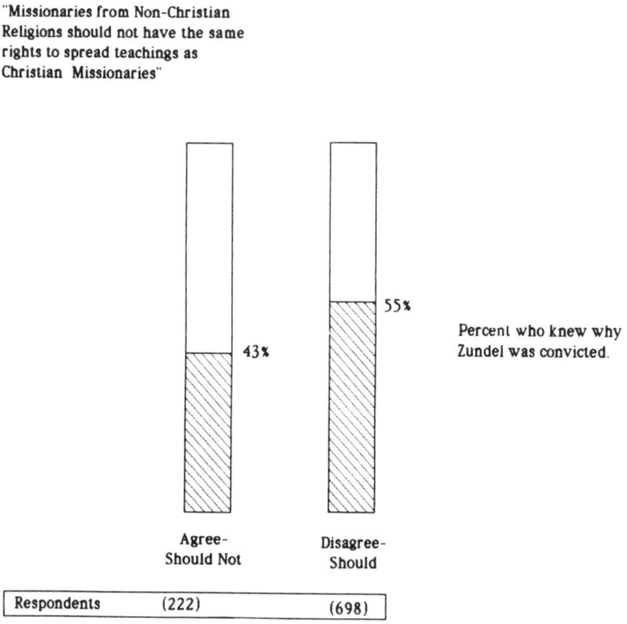

Interpretation: Religiously intolerant people were less aware of the trial.

Holocaust Attitudes

Another way of analysing how anti-Judaism may have been affected by the trial is to examine the relationship between knowledge of the trial and views about the Holocaust. Were Canadians more likely to accept the Nazi view of the Holocaust if they were aware of the trial? Our survey contained two questions about the Holocaust. Our Holocaust questions appeared to be concerned with facts but were actually about attitudes:

1. *"Thinking back to the treatment of the Jews in Europe, before and during World War II, do you think the persecution of the Jews was mostly the fault of the Jews, partly the fault of the Jews, or not at all the fault of the Jews?" and*
2. *"According to official estimates, about six million Jews were killed in the Holocaust. Do you think this estimate is too high, about right, or too low?"*

Fig. 2.4 displays the relationship between respondents' awareness of the trial and their views about who was to blame for the victimization of European Jews. Fig. 2.5 displays the relationship between awareness of the trial and respondents' opinions about how many Jews were killed. Who was to blame and how many were killed – these were central issues raised by Zundel at the trial. If Zundel was successful, it would be reasonable to expect his views to be shared more closely by people who were aware of the trial than by those who were unaware. However, the pattern revealed in our poll is the opposite. *Awareness of the trial was higher among Canadians who opposed Zundel's views than among those who shared them.*

One of Zundel's principal claims was that six million did not die. About one out of eight respondents expressed the view that fewer than six million actually perished. Among these particular respndents, only 42% were aware of the trial. By contrast, among respondents who believed that six million or more had perished, the proportion who were aware of the trial was 61%, i.e. one and a half times higher.

Zundel expressed the view that Jews themselves were responsible for their own deaths. Respondents who blamed Jews for their own misfortune were less apt to be aware of the trial than people who said that Jews were not at fault (47% vs. 58%). Here we have another hint that the trial may not have encouraged anti-Judaism. The trial may not have contributed to anti-Judaism for the simple reason that the events of the trial did not reach those who are most open to anti-Jewish thoughts.

Fig 2.4

Knowledge of the Trial and Responsibility for the Holocaust

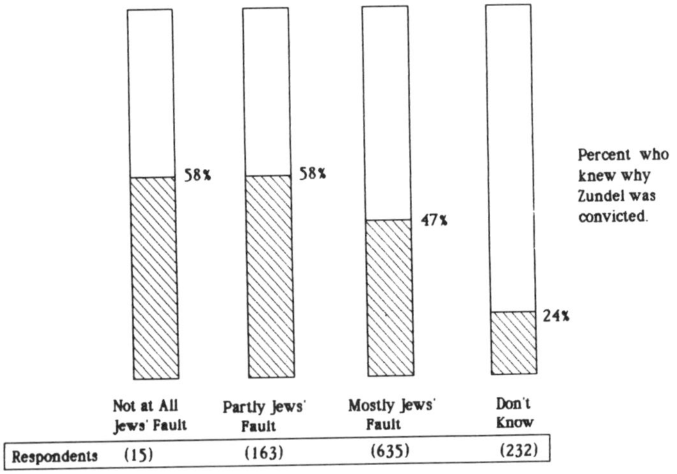

Interpretation: People who blamed Jews as well as those who did not know whom to blame tended to be unaware of the trial.

Fig 2.5

Knowledge of the Trial and Estimated Casualties

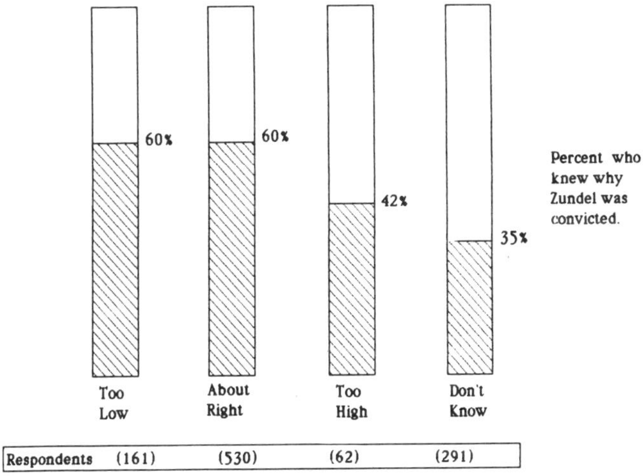

Interpretation: People who thought the "six million" estimate too high or had no opinion were less knowledgeable of the trial.

The most striking pattern in fig. 2.5. and especially fig. 2.4 is that those Canadians who were undecided about the Holocaust were least aware of the trial. Altogether, almost one out of every four Canadians did not know who was responsible for the persecution of European Jews. Almost one in three Canadians said that he or she did not know whether the six million estimate is too high, too low, or about right. These who did not know whether Jews were at fault for their own victimization were almost twice as likely to be oblivious of the trial as those who considered Jews to be innocent (75% vs. 42%). Those who said that they did not know the number of Jewish casualties were much more apt to be unaware of the trial than those who accepted the prevailing estimate (65% vs. 39%).

The "don't know" answers to the question about responsibilty for the Holocaust and about the magnitude of casualties can be interpreted as camouflaged opinion. "Not knowing" if six million Jews were liquidated may be an acknowledgement of ignorance or it may be a statement of opinion, questioning the validity of official estimates or it may be both in combination.

To summarize to this point, those respondents who were unaware of Zundel's trial provide the most fertile soil for his ideas. Those unaware of the trial were more likely to reveal ignorance of the simple facts of the Holocaust and were more likely to express Holocaust-related hostility to Jews.

Our survey contained measures of anti-Judaism which are unrelated to the Holocaust. For example, we asked *"Would you say that Jews have too much power, just enough, or not enough power in Canada?"* This is a longstanding and accepted way of measuring ethnic hostility or ethnocentricism. Although the question may appear to measure the power of Jews, it actually measures positve or negative feelings towards Jews. Whether or not Jews are too powerful is related to Ernst Zundel's claim that they constitute a world conspiracy.

A group which is in fact weak can be perceived as "too powerful" if it is considered very illegitimate. By the same token a strong group can be perceived as having just the right amount of power if it is thought to be legitimate. For example, almost half the American public thought that Jews were too powerful in the period immediately after the Holocaust. In fact, American Jews were so weak that they had been able to do very little to help their European co-religionists. As various professions and the universities were opened to Jews in the 1950's and 1960's, the proportion of Americans who considered Jews too powerful declined strongly. In the 1970's, the American public was much more apt to consider black Americans than Japanese Americans as too powerful. Yet, Japanese Americans were for years statistically over-represented in the professions, in the universities, in the mass media, and in other high earning occupations while blacks were under-represented.

Our statistical analysis revealed no relationship between attitudes about Jewish power and awareness of the trial. Those who believed that Jews have too much power were no more or less aware of the trial than those who thought that Jews had too little or just the right amount of power. The cardinal finding is that people familiar with the trial were *less* likely to express Holocaust-based anti-Judaism than people unfamiliar with the trial but they were *just as* likely to express another form of anti-Judaism. This finding hints at the possibility that the trial may have had a narrow educational effect in teaching Canadians what really happened in Europe. In general, the survey data showed that Holocaust-related anti-Judaism results from ignorance or hatred or both.

Comparing the Eichmann and Zundel Trials

To this point, our analysis has discussed only the impact of a single trial in a single country. Yet, case studies leave many questions unanswered. For example, is it normal for only half of the Canadian population to be aware of the trial given the intensive press coverage given to the event? A comparison of the public response to the Zundel trial with the public response to the Eichmann trial can help answer this and other questions.

The notorious SS was the elite military wing of the Nazi party and German state. The SS provided the state with the Death Head units to control the annihilation camps and the *Einsatzgruppen* (special-duty groups), which followed in the wake of victorious German armies. The task of the *Einsatzgruppen* was to hunt down as many real and fantasied enemies of National Socialism as possible. The *Einsatzgruppen* were a wing of the SS's special security service. Adolf Eichmann joined the SS's security service in 1934 as its "expert" on Zionism. Within a few years, he would acquire chief administrative responsibility for organizing the extermination of Europe's Jewish population.[11] In 1960, fifteen years after war's end, the Israeli intelligence service tracked him down in Buenos Aires, Argentina, and spirited him off to Jerusalem for trial.

By the middle of 1961, the Eichmann trial had occupied the world's headlines for more than a year. The events of the Nazi's capture and the circumstances of his trial were reported, analysed, and debated in the world media. Scholars carried out several attitude surveys and other kinds of studies of the public response to the trial. Four months before the court proceedings reached a conclusion, a Gallup poll showed that 87% of the United States population had heard of the trial.[12] Just before the trial's end, three American sociologists conducted an in depth regional survey in Oakland, California. The Oakland sample of 463 adults showed that virtually everyone claimed familiarity with the trial. Only 16% of respondents acknowledged having *never* heard of the trial. Yet, when the responses to the Oakland survey were examined more closely, the American respondents seemed less informed than at first glance.[13]

The Oakland, California questionnaire contained four specific measures of awareness of Eichmann's capture and trial. Respondents were asked: (1) *"In what country was Eichmann arrested?"* (2) *"What country arrested him?"*, (3) *"Do you know whether Eichmann was a Communist, Nazi, or a Jew?"*, and (4) *"What is the official estimate of the number of Jews killed by the Nazis?"* The California respondents revealed a considerable lack of knowledge of all the relevant issues. Only 27% knew that Eichmann was captured in Argentina. Only 42% knew that the State of Israel had apprehended him. Only 50% knew that he was a Nazi. Twelve percent thought that he was either a Communist or a Jew. Some of the 50% who replied correctly that Eichmann was a Nazi may simply have guessed.[14]

The California study asked respondents to comment on official estimates of the number of Jews killed in Europe. Only 28% agreed with the official estimate. The American researchers reached the following conclusion: "The impression conveyed by looking at the responses, question by question, is that *the trial did not penetrate very broadly or deeply* into the minds of the sample population . . . A picture emerges that may seem to many, distressing indeed."[15]

Eichmann, his capture, and his trial were far more momentous events that the prosecution of Cabbagetown's resident publisher of hate literature. Eichmann was a documented mass murderer who had cunningly eluded his pursuers for fifteen years. Israeli secret agents captured and removed him without the knowledge or cooperation of Argentina, which had for long contended with a strong homegrown fascist movement and an influential German expatriot community. Eichmann was put on trial in Jerusalem, ancient symbol of the people he sought to exterminate and capital of the country re-established on the rubble of Eichmann's Holocaust. Eichmann's capture and trial had the true makings of high drama. Yet, the Americans surveyed were no more aware – perhaps even less aware – of the Eichmann trial than Canadians were aware of the Zundel trial. Half of Canadians could say in their own words why Zundel was charged. Asked who Eichmann was, half of the Americans chose the Nazi option, but some may simply have guessed. Only 28% of the American respondents knew that six million had perished as compared to 51% among Canadians.

There are limits to how much the American reaction to the Eichmann trial can be compared to the Canadian reaction to the Zundel trial. The two studies did not employ the same question to measure public awareness or knowledge of the trial, and the American project did not involve a national sample of respondents. Nonetheless, the Eichmann study is the only existing study with which our findings can be compared. The Eichmann study demonstrated a very low level of awareness of the trial among the Americans interviewed. In view of the low level of knowledge among the American sample, the moderate level of awareness of the Zundel trial among Canadians acquires a different meaning. The 50% of Canadians who knew why Zundel was convicted becomes an indicator of substantial public interest. Civil libertarian Alan Borovoy, editor Rober Fulford, Tory columnist Dalton Camp and other concerned observers were right to declare that the trial would have an impact on the Canadian public. The Americans' ignorance of the Eichmann trial teaches us to lower the threshold for deciding when a public event has made a significant impact on the public imagination.

The American public's response to the Eichmann trial is useful not only for throwing light on Canadians' awareness of the Zundel trial but also for comparing those groups in society who were well informed with those who were ignorant. The American researchers found – as we did – that knowledge of the issues was much higher among people with considerable education, high incomes, and prestigious occupations. The Americans too found that men were more apt to be informed than women (52% vs. 37% as compared to 56% vs. 44% among Canadians).

In both the American and Canadian cases, the very people who are more apt to harbor unfriendly attitudes towards Jews – mainly the uneducated – are the people who are least likely to know about the trial and about the related Holocaust events. Scholars have shown a timeless pattern whereby the less educated members of society are more ill-informed about major public events in general, not merely important court trials but even simple items of news such as the name of the current President or Prime Minister.

The American scholars did not carry out a national survey on the impact of the Eichmann trial whereas we were able to do so in Canada. In our Canadian study, regional and linguistic differences in knowledge of the Zundel trial emerged in striking fashion. The difference in the degree of awareness between English and French Canadians and between Eastern and non-Eastern Canadians were as great as the differences between elementary school leavers and university graduates in *both* the American and Canadian cases. These vital linguistic and geographic differences will be explored in some detail in later chapters.

[1] Our analysis of the content of broadcasts focussed on television and on CBC television in particular. Television news attracts a greater audience and exercises a greater impact than radio news with respect to non-local events. CBC news attracts a greater audience and exercises a greater impact than CTV and the other private broadcasters. Finally, CBC television news maintains good machine-readable records of its program content and was prepared to offer this information to us.

[2] Our comments on the audience for Canadian news are based on the research of the CBC as reported in various written submissions to the Canadian Radio-Television Telecommunications Commission.

[3] Telephone conversation, June, 1985, our translation from the French.

[4] Because our limited research resources did not permit the analysis of radio news content, we did not ask respondents about their use of this particular medium.

[5] Doris Graber, *Processing the News: How People Tame the Information Tide* (New York: Longman, 1984).

[6] The Zundel trial was not the only issue which penetrated the consciousness of only half of Canada's population. Gallup asked Canadians if they had "heard or read anything about the racial policies followed by the government in South Africa." Although the media had provided weeks of coverage of the unrest and violence in the country, only one out of two Canadians acknowledged awareness of the issue. *Citizen* (August 22nd., 1985), p. A3

[7] Because of Prince Edward Island's small population, most national surveys interview few respondents on the Island and these respondents are normally lumped together with Nova Scotians. We followed this practice.

[8] Richard Hamilton, *Who Voted for Hitler* (Princeton: Princeton University Press, 1982) and Irving Abella and Harold Troper, *None Is Too Many* (Toronto: Lester & Orpen Denys, 1982). See also Lita-Rose Betcherman, *The Swastika and the Maple Leaf* (Toronto: Fitzhenry and Whiteside, 1975).

[9] See Werner Cohn, "English and French Canadian Public Opinion on Jews and Israel: Some Poll Data", *Canadian Ethnic Studies* (1979), 31-48.

[10] Charles Y. Glock and Rodney Stark, *Christian Beliefs and Anti-Semitism* (New York: Harper and Row, 1966).

[11] See Lucy S. Dawidowicz, *The War Against the Jews, 1933-1945* (New York: Holt, Rinehart and Winston, 1975).

[12] For this item and for other evidence about the impact on the U.S. public, see Charles Y. Glock, Gertrude J. Selznick, and Joe L. Spaeth, *The Apathetic Majority: a Study Based on Public Responses to the Eichmann Trial* (New York: Harper and Row, 1966).

[13] ibid.

[14] pp. 27-28.

[15] p. 27, our emphasis.

Chapter 3

The Impact of the Trial

The central purpose of this study has been to assess whether the trial produced a "boomerang" effect. For a major boomerang effect to have occurred, a large proportion of Canadians ought to have been aware of the trial. The preceding chapter showed that only half of Canada's inhabitants were aware of the trial. Noting the kinds of people who were aware of the trial as opposed to those who were not, the chapter pointed to the possibility that the trial may not have affected public opinion in the way feared by many commentators.

Our survey contained several questions designed to measure the impact of the trial on respondents' feelings. The single most direct question was the following: *"Has the Zundel trial made you feel more sympathetic or less sympathetic towards Jews?"* A similarly worded question was also asked in order to help reveal how attitudes towards Germans might have been affected. Asking people if a major event changed their feelings about a group of people is not a perfect way of finding out if the event did in fact change their feelings. For example, people who were sympathetic to Jews from the outset might report becoming more sympathetic as a result of Zundel whereas in fact they may have simply remained highly sympathetic as before. People hostile to Jews may report no change in affection since, from their perspective, the Holocaust denial voiced in the courtroom justified their longstanding animosity. Inspite of the limitations of our survey question, the answers to this question can be revealing. We had at our disposal some ways of circumventing the weakness of the question, as we shall show in a moment.

According to the testimony of our respondents, the trial did not affect the feelings of most people but was much more likely to increase than to decrease sympathy for Jews. Half (47%) of the respondents said that their feelings towards Jews remained unchanged. One-fourth (26%) reported that they did not know how their feelings were affected while one fourth (24%) said that they became more sympathetic. Only a negligible number (2%) reported a reverse effect, i.e. becoming less sympathetic to Jews (see fig. 3.1).

Fig 3.1

Change in Sympathy towards Jews:
All Respondents

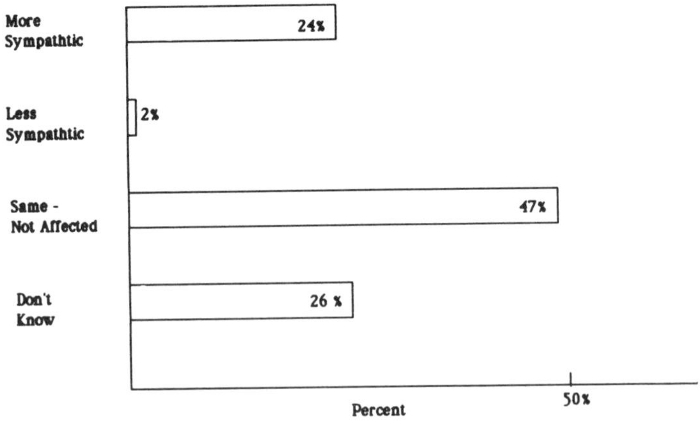

Number of respondents 1045

Interpretation: The number of people saying that they became more sympathetic as a result of the trial was much larger than the number saying that they became less sympathetic.

Fig 3.2

Change in Sympathy towards Jews,
Only Among Respondents Knowledgeable of the Trial.

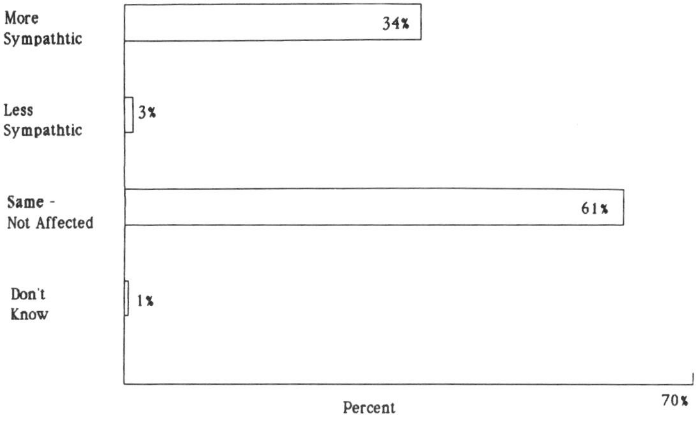

Number of respondents 527

Interpretation: The number of people saying that they became more sympathetic as a result of the trial was much larger than the number saying that they became less sympathetic.

It is possible that some of those who reported no change in their sympathy for Jews as a result of the trial were simply too unaware of the trial to be affected by it. To explore this possibility, we focussed on those who were well informed about the case, i.e. those who knew why Zundel was convicted. The proportion of all Canadians who did not know how their feelings were affected by the trial was one-fourth as contrasted with only 2% among those who followed the trial (see figs. 3.1 and 3.2). It is not surprising that those who did not know about the trial tended not to know how the trial had affected their feelings. Indeed, the fact that virtually all of those who knew why Zundel was convicted knew how their feelings had been affected suggests that asking respondents about the reason for the conviction was an effective way of identifying those whose feelings were influenced by the event.

Respondents were more apt to say that they became more sympathetic to Jews if they followed the trial than if they did not. The proportion who reported becoming more sympathetic to Jews was 34% among people who were aware of the trial as compared to 24% among Canadians as a whole. Whether or not people were aware of the trial, the proportion saying that they had become less sympathetic to Jews remained negligible.

Given that Canadians said that they were much more likely to feel more favourable towards Jews as a result of the trial, how did the trial affect their attitudes towards Germans? To see if the trial had affected attitudes towards Germans, interviewers asked respondents the following question, *"Has the Zundel trial made you feel more sympathetic or less sympathetic towards Germans?"* Once again, most people said that their views remained unchanged or that they did not know how their views had changed. But, among those reporting a change, far more people reported becoming less sympathetic rather than more sympathetic (14% vs. 4%: see fig. 3.3). The tendency to become less sympathetic towards Germans was especially strong among those who were aware of the trial (see fig. 3.4). Among Canadians who knew why Zundel had been convicted, virtually everyone reported knowing how the trial had affected his/her feelings towards Germans. The largest group continued to report no change in feelings. But, among those whose feelings had changed, the anti-Germans outnumbered the pro-Germans by a ratio of three-to-one (16% vs. 5%).

To summarize to this point, the largest group of Canadians reported no change in feelings towards Jews or Germans. The relative proportion of "no changes" and "don't knows" diminished sharply as we focussed on those Canadians who could recall what the trial was about. Many newspaper commentators feared that Zundel would be successful in his avowed goal of using the courtroom as a platform for disseminating hate against Jews. *In fact, he was more successful in disseminating animosity against Germans.* Among respondents reporting a change of sympathy, 92% reported an *increase* in sympathy for Jews while 79% reported a *decrease* in sympathy for Germans.

The animosity against Germans aroused by the trial is explained partly by the fact that Zundel himself was a German national and partly by the fact that responsibility for the Holocaust rested mainly with the German state. Zundel made no secret of his identification with and love for Germany. This fact may go some distance in accounting for the increase in anti-German sentiment among the Canadian public. Had a survey asked Canadians the same question after the conviction of the Canadian-born James Keegstra, it might have shown that Keegstra's conviction aroused less anti-German feeling.

The way in which the mass media reported both the trial and Holocaust news unrelated to the trial may have contributed to anti-German feeling as well. The media focussed on the death camps and on the role of the German state in their creation and operation. With the notable exception of the CBC Journal's special series on the Holocaust collaboration of Vichy France aired in 1984, the media generally avoided a discussion of the role of the Axis powers, the peoples conquered by them, and the behaviour of the Allies. The absence of a cross-national perspective may have left innocent media consumers the mistaken impression that anti-Judaism was mainly or exclusively a German problem. Furthermore, the absence of historical perspective may have left some media consumers with the impression that anti-Judaism began with the birth of the Nazi party.

The relative absence of cross-national and historical perspective in Holocaust stories results from the customary methods of operation of the press and television. Both media focus on recent, discrete events, rather than an unfolding process of events which may have taken place sometime ago. Newspapers attract readers by offering clearly written reports on the essential facts of yesterday's news, not by offering comprehensive accounts of complex events which took place decades earlier. Television news attracts viewers, especially the marginal clients for news, by offering dramatic visual footage, not by offering profound and therefore longwinded analyses of complex phenomena. It is difficult for broadcasters and newspapers seeking mass audiences to offer the same degree of comprehensiveness, subtlety and therefore objectivity which may be expected of university history courses.

Fig 3.3

Change in Sympathy towards Germans:
All Respondents

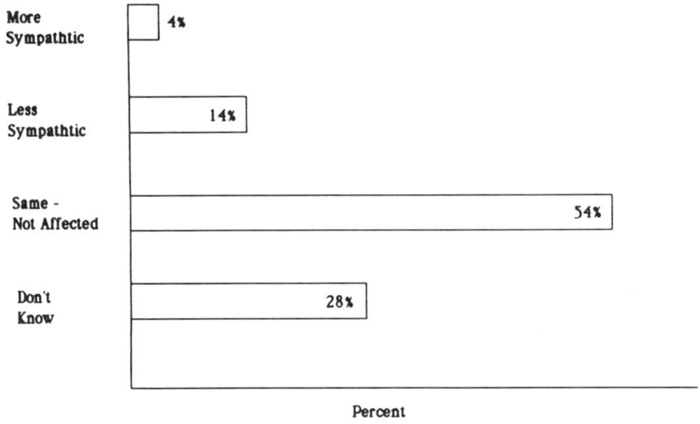

Number of
respondents
1043

Interpretation: The number of people saying that they became more sympathetic as a result of the trial was much less than the number saying that they became less sympathetic.

Fig 3.4

Change in Sympathy towards Germans,
Only Among Respondents Knowledgeable of the Trial

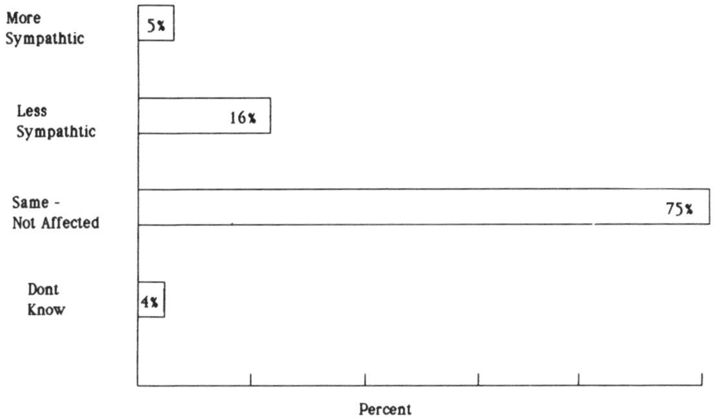

Number of respondents 526

Interpretation: The number of people saying that they became more sympathetic as a result of the trial was much less than the number saying that they became less sympathetic.

Attitudes towards Jews – Who Changed?

What kinds of people became more sympathetic to Jews and what kinds were unaffected by the trial or became less sympathetic? Although few in number, those who became less sympathetic to Jews are relatively easy to describe. Those few who reported becoming less sympathetic were similar in profile to those kinds of people who were most apt to be unaware that the trial took place. In the category of people who became less sympathetic were francophones, people of limited education, young people, and respondents living in Newfoundland or Alberta. We are unable to say how the increased negative feelings among a minority of Albertans may have been related to the difficulties in Eckville. Ex-history teacher James Keegstra and his friends may have succeeded in disseminating their racist views among a minority of Albertans. Or, Keegstra and his friends may have reflected a facet of Alberta's once strong Social Credit movement. A Social Credit fringe group had occasionally produced a bizarre mixture of anti-Communist, anti-capitalist, anti-secular, anti-Jewish, and anti-Catholic rhetoric.[1]

Those respondents in our national survey who reported becoming more sympathetic to Jews were similar to those who were aware of the trial in that they tended to be English-speakers and residents of British Columbia, Saskatchewan or Ontario. Residents of these three provinces tended to follow the trial and, whether or not they followed the trial, tended to become more sympathetic to Jews (see table 3.1). Elderly people (those over 60), high school graduates, and women tended also to become more sympathetic. Although women were less informed of the trial than men, women reported becoming more sympathetic to Jews than did men.

People who said that their feelings about Jews remained unchanged tended to be males, younger than 60 years old, anglophones, university educated, and residents of Alberta and Nova Scotia. The unchanging response of university graduates makes sense since these people were most apt to be well informed about the Holocaust before the trial began. Even those university graduates who were not previously informed might not wish to reveal that their feelings had changed and thereby acknowledge indirectly that they had not been terribly knowledgeable before.

Table 3.1
Changes in Sympathy Towards Jews
by Province
(column percentages)

	Nfld.	N.S.	N.B.	Que.	Ont.	Man.	Sask.	Alta.	B.C.	Row Total
More sympathetic	13	20	20	17	28	25	32	20	35	25%
Less sympathetic	7	0	0	1	2	3	4	7	0	2%
Same — not affected	13	60	33	35	53	43	60	59	53	47%
Don't know	68	20	48	47	17	30	4	14	12	26%
Column Total	100% (31)	100% (30)	100% (40)	100% (264)	100% (369)	100% (40)	100% (50)	100% (99)	100% (122)	

The Impacts of the Eichmann and Zundel Trials

The impact of the Eichmann trial on sympathy for Jews reveals some similarity with the Zundel trial. Neither conviction produced a "boomerang" or negative effect. Virtually the same numbers of Canadians and Americans reported that their feelings remained unchanged - 46% vs. 47%. The same percentage - 2% - reported becoming less sympathetic to Jews in each case. Half of the respondents in both cases said that their feelings had remained unchanged by events. In the Zundel case, we showed that almost all of those whose feelings had been unaffected by the trial were those who had been unaware of the trial. Perhaps in the Eichmann case, too, those who were unmoved were unaware.

One difference between the two trials is that the Americans were more apt than the Canadians to indicate sympathy for Jews - 37% vs. 24%. The greater indication of sympathy for Jews in the Eichmann case may stem from the nature of the defendant. Eichmann planned and administered murder on a vast scale. He was a major actor in history. To say that he was a mass murderer does not do justice to the magnitude of his evil. Zundel was a minor publicist and propagandist. At his worst, it can be said of Zundel that he sought to create a climate of opinion in which the murder of Jews would be viewed as justifiable.

The greater sympathy elicited by the Eichmann trial may also stem from differences in national cultures. Jews and Judaism have long occupied a slightly less pejorative place in American culture for reasons having to do with the religious roots of early Pilgrim settlement. The Puritans were fugitives from religious persecution who identified with other victims of religious oppression. As "Old Testament" men and women, the Puritans saw themselves as early Israelites fleeing the oppression of Egypt's Pharoah. For the Puritans, Europe was Egypt. The Atlantic ocean was the Sinai desert. America was the promised land, Zion, the new Jerusalem. The Puritans, it may be remembered, were the theological descendents of Oliver Cromwell, under whose rule England readmitted Jews after a long period of exclusion. Cromwell's supporters contemplated adopting Hebrew as England's national language and returning the sabbath to Saturday. The Puritans of New England searched throughout the Old Testament or Hebrew Bible for ways of giving meaning to their experience. At the Continental Congress in 1776, Benjamin Franklin proposed for the Great Seal a portrait of Moses dividing the Red Sea and the Pharoah drowning while Thomas Jefferson proposed a portrait of the children of Israel struggling through the wilderness.

The Hebraic theological roots of early America led to laws and practices which made life in America somewhat less oppressive for Jews than in Europe. Rhode Island and other states settled by the Puritans led in the granting of equal voting and citizenship rights to Jews. By the middle of the 19th century, the United States government was the principal international spokesman for oppressed Jewish minorities in central and Eastern Europe. A century before Presidents Jimmy Carter and Ronald Reagan would ask the Kremlin to permit Russian Jews to emigrate, Washington was asking the Czar to bring an end to pogroms (massacres). In the 19th century, a significant minority of American Protestants were active proponents of zionism.[2]

Before dwelling at too great a length on the possible cultural differences between the two countries, it is important to realize that English Canadians are not as different from Americans as our survey data seem to imply. The main reason why only 24% of Canadians reported an increased sympathy for Jews is the relative lack of sympathy for Jews among French Canadians. As many as 37% indicated increased sympathy in the American study as compared to 31% among respondents in the English-speaking provinces and 17% in Quebec. We shall return to a discussion of French-speaking Canadians later in our analysis.

Anti-Judaism Before and After the Trial

Above, we examined the attitudinal impact of the Canadian trial by analysing the changed sympathies of respondents as reported by the respondents themselves. Yet, it is an axiom in the social sciences that people should not always be believed. Respondents may not be conscious of how their feelings have changed. Alternately, they may be fully aware of their feelings and consciously choose not to tell the truth. In order to overcome the liability of relying on what respondents tell us, we resorted to an additional method.

Our survey asked respondents the following question: *"Would you say that Jews have too much power, just enough power, or not enough power in Canada?"* Asking this question after the trial enabled us to see if the trial had made a difference in the magnitude of anti-Judaism because the very same question had been asked before. The League for Human Rights of B'nai Brith had set out to study anti-Judaism in Canada during the early 1980's. In 1983 and again in 1984, the League carried out nation-wide surveys with samples of 2011 and 2038 people.[3]

Table 3.2 and fig. 3.5 compare the responses of Canadian adults to the very same question in the years 1983 and 1984, before the trial, and in 1985, just after the conviction. Such a year-to-year comparison is one of the better ways to measure the trial's overall impact because it is more immune to misleading answers by respondents. The risk of asking people at one point in time how they had felt in the past is that they may not remember their previous feelings with much accuracy. The three years of data support the main thrust of our earlier contention, namely that the trial did not increase the magnitude of anti-Jewish feeling in Canada.

The distribution of anti-Jewish opinions did not change significantly from 1983 to 1984 or from 1984 to 1985. In 1985, the proportion of people who thought that Jews held too much power appeared to increase by three percentage points, from 12% to 15%. However, this change is within the range of sampling error or chance variation. The apparent increase in anti-Judaism in 1985 may be more apparent than real. The increase of 3% may be too small to deserve mention just as the decrease of 2% in the previous year is may also be too small to be interpreted as more than a sampling accident. The fact that 12-15% of the Canadian people are anti-Jewish may be alarming, but this proportion appears stable and unaffected by the Zundel trial.

In September, 1985, after both the Zundel and Keegstra trials, the League for Human Rights of B'nai Brith carried out its regular annual survey of ethnocentricism. The survey found that 16% of Canadians perceived Jews to be too powerful. The September, 1985 figure of 16% is 1% higher than our March, 1985 figure, 4% higher than in 1984, and 2% higher than in 1983. The 15%-16% figures for 1985 may be interpreted in a number of different ways. First, the 15%-16% figures for 1985 may be only chance variations of no fundamental importance. Secondly, the 15%-16% figures in 1985 may be short-term fluctuations, reflecting the momentary irritation of some Canadians at the relatively high volume of Jewish news in the media. Thirdly, the 15%-16% figures may reflect an actual increase in hardcore anti-Jewish prejudice in 1985, whatever the reason for this increase. Fourthly, the 15-16% figures may reflect an increase in hardcore anti-Jewish prejudice brought about by the hate trials.

Our analysis suggests that either the 15%-16% figures are chance variations or that a few Canadians were driven to express anti-Jewish prejudice by their irritation at the volume of Jewish news in the media. The League for Human Rights' September, 1985 survey yielded evidence that hardcore prejudice remained stable during the year. Respondents were asked if they would vote for a Jewish candidate of their favourite political party. The responses in autumn, 1985 were almost identical to those given in 1984.[4] Our own data suggest furthermore that the Zundel trial did not increase anti-Jewish prejudice. Those respondents who followed the trial were less prejudiced than those who did not. Among those respondents reporting that their feelings about Jews were affected by the trial, an overwhelming majority reported becoming more sympathetic.

The proportion of Canadians who believe that Jews have too much power is comparable to current American figures. In the mid-1960's, a national U.S. study reported that 11% of respondents believed that Jews are too powerful. This was a marked decline from the 44% of Americans who thought that Jews were too powerful in the late 1940's, shortly after the Holocaust.[5]

Fig. 3.5
Annual Changes in Perceived Power of Jews

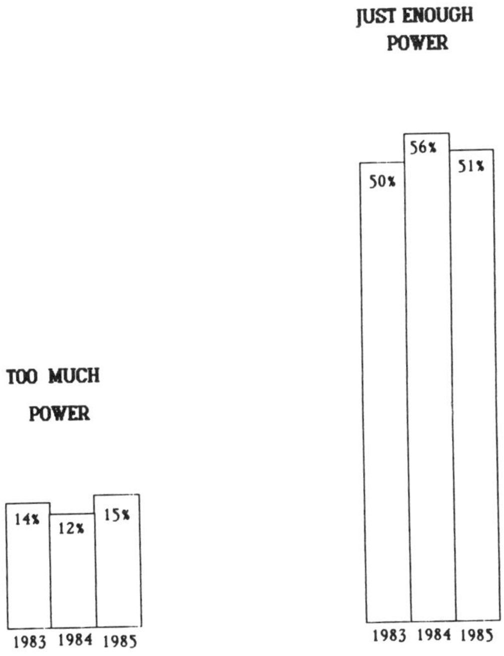

Interpretation: Anti-Jewish prejudice did not rise in the year of the trial more than can be expected as a result of chance variations in the measurement of opinion by poll.

Table 3.2
Perceived Power of Jews in Canada, 1983-85

	1983	1984	1985
Too much power	14	12	15
Just enough	50	56	51
Not enough	6	5	6
Don't know	26	25	27
Not states	4	2	1
	100%	100%	100%
	(2011)	(2038)	(1054)

Source: *The Review of Anti-Semitism in Canada, 1984* for 1983 and 1984 data.

The 12-16% of respondents who believe that Jews are too powerful is comparable to the findings on this subject which were unearthed by Goldfarb Consultants, the survey research firm.[6] Martin Goldfarb's firm conducted a national survey in 1984 on behalf of the Canada-Israel Committee to determine attitudes towards Jews, Israel, and the Middle East. Given 1000 respondents, the questionnaire included questions on the perceived influence of Jews in business, politics, the media, government, and a category called "wealth and resources." The proportion of Canadians who felt that Jews have too much power varied from 11% to 22% depending on the field. Eleven percent believed that Jews have too much influence in the media and government as compared to 12% in politics, 19% in wealth and resources, and 22% in business.

Holocaust Denial

Another method of measuring the impact of the trial is to explore if Canadians are beginning to doubt whether the Holocaust took place as described in official government documents and in the studies conducted by scholars. Readers may recall that Zundel used the prolonged trial to cast repeated doubt on the Holocaust. Day after day, in court, the unbelievable questions were repeated. Did the Holocaust really happen? Did six million really die? Were there gas chambers? Did smoke come out of the chimneys? Could zyklon

B (i.e. cyanide) really kill people? These questions were central to Zundel's leaflet, *Did Six Million Really Die?,* and his many other publications. They were raised in the courtroom by the defendant's lawyer, Douglas Christie, and then reported coast-to-coast in the Canadian media.

One of the purposes of raising doubts about the Holocaust was simply to make the case that it had not occurred or that the conventional understanding was enormously exaggerated. Another conceivable purpose of raising doubts about the Holocaust was to arouse the hostility against Jews, to suggest that they fabricated the whole event for personal gain or to suggest that whatever misfortune they actually did experience was of their own doing. We asked the following question:

> *"Do you think that the persecution of the Jews was mostly their fault, partly their fault, or not at all their fault?"*

A large minority chose an apparently neutral or a clearly unsympathetic answer to this question. *Only 60% of Canadians held Jews blameless for their dispossession and murder during World War II.* As many as 16% said that it was "partly" their own fault. Almost one-fourth – 23% – stated that they did not know how to apportion responsibility.

We also sought people's views about the magnitude of casualties. The question was worded as follows:

> *"According to official estimates six million Jews were killed in the Holocaust. Do you think this estimate is too high, about right or too low?"*

Once again, a large minority chose an apparently neutral or clearly unsympathetic answer. *Barely half of Canadians agreed that six million Jews actually died.* Fifteen percent believed that the estimate was too high. Another 28% indicated that they did not know. These are indeed unpleasant findings, but they are not a consequence of the Zundel trial.

We compared people who were aware of the trial and people who were not with respect to how they assigned responsibility for the Holocaust and how they felt about the estimate of six million. Fig. 3.6 shows that people who were aware of the trial were *less* likely to express anti-Jewish views. The proportion of Canadians who agreed that the official estimate of six million deaths was right was only 40% among those unaware of the trial but as high as 61% among those who were aware. Those who either blamed Jews or who believed that fewer than six million died were apt to be unable to explain why Zundel's trial took place. Those Canadians who believed that reports about the Holocaust were exaggerated and who therefore were potentially most receptive to Holocaust-denial propaganda held their views before the trial took place. Those most receptive to Holocaust-denial propaganda were not affected by the trial because they were unaware of it.

Fig. 3.6

Knowledge of the Trial and Doubts about Holocaust

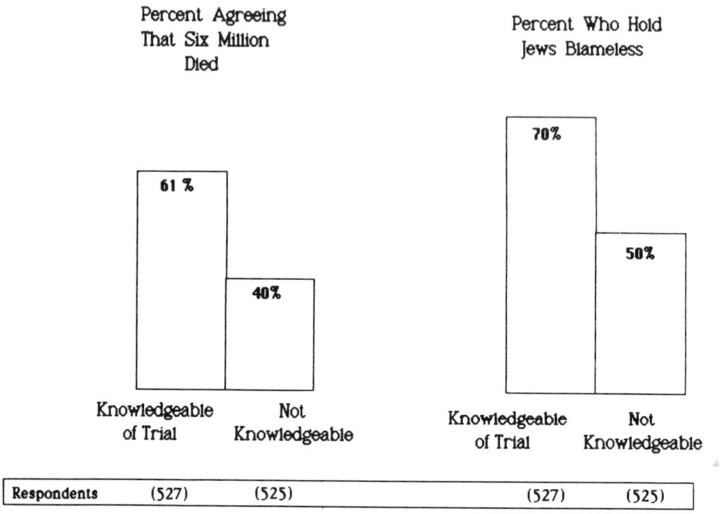

Interpretation: People knowledgeable of the trial were more likely to agree that six million died and Jews were blameless.

Table 3.3
Holocaust Doubts after Eichmann and Zundel Trials

	After Eichmann Trial - Total Sample	After Zundel Trial - Total Sample	After Zundel Trial - Only Those Aware
Jewish Persecution			
partly Jews' fault	30	16	18
mostly Jews' fault	+ 2 =32	+ 1 =17	+ 1 =19
not all Jews' fault	53	60	70
Don't know	15	23	11
	100%	100%	100%
Official Estimate of Six Million is			
about right	36	50	61
too high	42	15	13
too low	13	6	7
don't know	9	28	19
	100%	100%	100%

A comparison with the Eichmann trial shows that Canadians today are more informed about the Holocaust than were Americans in the 1960's. Table 3.3 shows that Americans were more likely than Canadians to hold Jews responsible for their misfortune and more likely to believe that the estimate of six million is exaggerated. Thus, 32% of Americans held Jews at least partly responsible as compared to only 17% among Canadians. As many as 42% of American respondents in the American study believed that the six million estimate was too high as compared to only 15% among Canadians.

How can the greater willingness of Americans to blame Jews and to underestimate their human losses be reconciled with the evidence, discussed earlier, that Americans were more apt to report increased sympathy? On the one hand, a larger *majority* of Americans expressed feelings of increased sympathy. On the other hand, a larger *minority* of Americans than Canadians blamed Jews for their own misery and underplayed the loss of life. One possible explanation is that the American people are more polarized on the Jewish question as they often are on other questions. The greater polarization of the American respondents is one of a number of possible explanations for the different findings in the two studies. However, given the smaller size of the American sample of respondents and the fact that the American study was not national in scope, excessive effort should not be devoted to accounting for differences between the two countries which may be more apparent than real.

The "Climate of Doubt"

One of the paradoxes in the analysis of public opinion is that people may hold one opinion but believe - incorrectly sometimes - that other people hold another opinion. In elections, candidates can often give an impression of greater support than they actually have by the intensive use of campaign signs and the clever use of the mass media. To this point, we have shown that Canadians did not become more anti-Jewish as a result of the trial and its "one million dollars of free publicity." They did not begin to doubt the record of the Holocaust as a result of the urgings of the proponents of Holocaust denial. Among Canadians aware of the trial, fewer people said that they did not know how many Jews were killed and more people accepted the conventional record of the period. However, do Canadians believe that their fellow citizens also see the world as they do?

We asked respondents the following question: *"The media have talked a lot about the doubts and questions raised by Mr. Zundel over the past few weeks. In your opinion, are there a few Canadians, many Canadians, or almost no Canadians who now believe we should seriously question the historical records of this period?"* Fig. 3.7 portrays the distribution of responses to this question.

Most respondents feel that at least *some* other Canadians now have doubts. Thirteen percent believe that "many" people have doubts. As many as 30% believe that "a few" have doubts. Thirty-three percent do not know if other people have doubts. Fewer than one out of every four respondents - 23% - express the view that "almost no one" doubts the existence of the Holocaust.

It is difficult to know with confidence if the trial caused people to attribute doubts about the Holocaust to their fellow citizens. An ideal way of ascertaining whether the trial caused the doubts would be to compare our findings with reported doubts in national surveys carried out before the trial. However, previous national surveys did not ask Canadians if they thought that other people had doubts about the existence of the Holocaust. The existence of

Fig 3.7

How Many Canadians Now Believe That We Should Question the Record of the Holocaust?

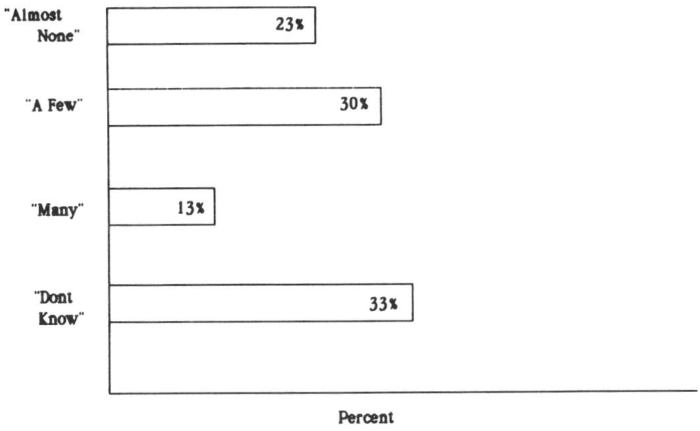

Number of respondents 1043

Interpretation: Most people think that the trial made at least "a few" people question the record of the Holocaust..

death camps was not widely debated in the media before Ernst Zundel was charged in the courts.

Our own data suggests that people were led to attribute doubts to other Canadians as a result of the trial. We compared the responses of those who knew what the trial was about with the responses of those who did not. *Those who knew why Zundel was convicted were almost twice as likely to attribute doubt to other people as those who did not know why he was convicted even though people who knew why he was convicted were much less likely to harbour doubts about the Holocaust themselves.* The proportion of respondents who thought that either "a few" or "many" Canadians would now have doubts about how the Holocaust occurred was as a high as 55% among those informed about the trial and only 31% among those who were uninformed.

When this finding is matched with our previously reported findings, we are able to create the following portrait of the overall impact of the trial. The trial increased somewhat public knowledge about the Holocaust and engendered greater sympathy for Jews while, at the same time, it led people to believe that their neighbours were moving in the opposite direction.

Of course, we cannot be totally and absolutely certain that the trial itself prompted people to believe that their neighbours now doubted the Holocaust. Canadians who were aware of the trial were not a cross-section of society. Readers will remember that Canadians knowledgeable of the trial tended to be English-speaking, well educated, older, male, and residents of British Columbia, Ontario, Saskatchewan. Perhaps people who were knowledgeable of the trial were pessimistic people who normally attributed doubt to other people or perhaps they were thinking about people with less education than themselves. We tried many varieties of statistical analysis to see if we could find any evidence for explanations for attributing doubt other than the trial. But, we could find no such evidence. People who were knowledgeable of the trial were in fact more likely to believe – incorrectly – that more Canadians now doubt the historical record of the Holocaust. The fact that our more informed respondents were apt to distrust their neighbours' ability to think helps to explain why the journalists and experts, discussed above in chapter 1, were so certain that the trial would be a propaganda coup for neo-Nazism.

Not all of the respondents aware of the trial iwere equally certain that the trial would engender doubts in the minds of their neighbours. The more pro-Jewish respondents showed a slight tendency to be more confident of their neighbours. Most respondents (61%) held Jews blameless for their victimization. Only 16% said that Jews were "party at fault" and only 1% said that they were "mostly at fault." Among Canadians who held Jews entirely blameless, 28% said that no one would doubt the record of the Holocaust. The corresponding figures were 20% and 13% among people who held Jews partly or wholly responsible. Half of our respondents (51%) thought that the accepted estimate of six million casualties was correct. Those who accepted the estimate were more likely to think that no one now doubts the record of the Holocaust than those who thought the estimate too high (30% vs. 18%).

At first glance, the fact that the trial made people misjudge their neighbours may seem unimportant. As long as the trial increased the public's understanding of the cataclysm, does it matter that people now think that their fellow citizens are moving in the opposite direction? The simple answer is that it does matter. It matters because people do not like to live in social isolation. People may fear being rejected socially or even being disadvantaged at work as a result of expressing unpopular beliefs. Initially, people who hold views which they perceive to be unpopular minority opinions may hesitate to share these views in public. Eventually, they may moderate their views or lose interest in the subject. People who belong to the initial minority may be emboldened to express their views more often and with greater enthusiasm as they observe the reticence of the majority. People who initially have no strong opinion may gradually adopt the views which they hear expressed more often and which they perceive to be the most popular and therefore the most convincing. As a result of these processes, opinions which were once held only by a minority can in due course become the opinion of the majority.[7] In the particular case of the Zundel affair, if people continue to believe – for the moment, wrongly – that their neighbours acquired doubts about the Holocaust, more and more doubts would be expressed about the Holocaust and the "revisionist" perspective would eventually prevail.[8]

The dangers of the "climate of doubt" are real. When people think that their neighbours have begun to doubt the official record of the Holocaust, they may begin to express doubts themselves. Our data show that Canadians who hold Jews blameless for the calamity are less apt to perceive their fellow citizens as doubters than do Canadians who blame Jews. How can we explain the link between blaming Jews for the Holocaust and believing that more Canadians now doubt the record of that period? It is possible that once people decide to hold Jews responsible for their victimization, they then jump to the conclusion that other people must also have reservations about the accepted view of this chapter in European history. However, it is also plausible that many people decide to hold Jews responsible after concluding that increasing numbers of Canadians are questioning the official record of this period.

In election campaigns, the "bandwagon effect" is the term used to describe how some voters cast their eyes about to discover which train will reach the station first and, then, jump aboard. Politicians use lawn signs, television commercials, and declarations of support from known personalities to persuade voters that their train is going to reach the station first. The mass media tell people which politicians are winning and which opinions are prevailing. The media are less influential on contemporary and local issues such as highway construction, where the average citizen can readily observe whether more roads are needed. But, the media are vital in issues such as the Holocaust which are far removed geographically and historically from the life experience of the average Canadian.

* * * * *

The trial of Ernst Zundel and the attendant publicity did not succeed in persuading Canadians of the virtues of Holocaust denial as feared by newspaper columnists, civil libertarians, Jewish leaders, and others worried about bringing him to rial. The trial did not penetrate very broadly into the mind of the public. Our single national survey yielded evidence that Canadians became more sympathetic to Jews. Respondents were much more likely to report becoming more sympathetic to Jews rather than less, especially in the case of respondents who were aware of the trial. Presumably, people who were already sympathetic or emotionally neutral before the trial became more sympathetic after. People aware of the trial were more likely to accept the historical record of the period and were more likely to hold Jews blameless for their persecution. But, people aware of the trial were more likely to think that their neighbours now had doubts about the Holocaust. A comparison with surveys conducted in 1983 and 1984 shows that the ranks of the prejudiced hardcore grew little, if at all. According to the data, if the prejudiced hardcore grew slightly, this was likely not a result of the Zundel trial.

Ironically, the propensity to deny the Holocaust was strongest among those unaware of the trial and therefore predated Zundel's intensive media exposure. The fact that anti-Jewish attitudes, including Holocaust denial, existed before the trial suggests that the broader sources of anti-Judaism in society should be explored. We look at some of these broader considerations in chapter 5. But, first we examine the media.

[1] C.B. MacPherson, *Democracy in Alberta* (Toronto: University of Toronto Press, 1962), 183-4 and Michael B. Stein, *The Dynamics of Right-Wing Protest* (Toronto: University of Toronto Press, 1973), 49-50. In September, 1985, after Keegstra's trial in Alberta, the League for Human Rights conducted a national survey to measure anti-Jewish and other ethnocentric sentiments. The survey results provided some evidence that the trial increased slightly anti-Jewish sentiments in that province. Respondents were asked, as in previous League surveys, if they would be willing to vote for a candidate for office who happened to be Jewish. Canadians as a whole were willing in 1985 as in 1984 to vote for a Jewish candidate, but Albertans were slightly less willing. Albertans were no less willing in 1985 than in 1984 to vote for candidates of other ethnic minorities. Our appreciation to Professors Stephen Scheinberg and Taylor Buckner for drawing this to our attention. A report on the September, 1985 dataset is to appear in a forthcoming issue of *The Review of Anti-Semitism in Canada.*

[2] For an extraordinary account of the Biblical appeal of zionism for American Protestants from John Adams to Harry Truman, see Peter Grose, *Israel in the Mind of America* (New York: Alfred A. Knopf, 1984).

[3] See H. Taylor Buckner, "A Study of Canadian Attitudes towards Jews, Italians, and Poles – A Preliminary Comparative Analysis, 1983 and 1984," *The Review of Anti-Semitism in Canada: 1984* (Downsview: League for Human Rights of B'nai Brith, 1985), table 7.

[4] Our appreciation to Professor Taylor Buckner, Professor Stephen Scheinberg, and Arthur Hiess for this information.

[5] See Gertrude J. Selznick and Stephen Steinberg, *The Tenacity of Prejudice: Anti-Semitism in Contemporary America* (New York: Harper and Row, 1969) and Nathan Perlmutter and Ruth Ann Perlmutter, *The Real Anti-Semitism in America* (New York: Arbor House, 1982).

[6] Goldfarb Consultants, "Perceptions of Jews, Israel and the Middle East," a research report prepared for the Canada-Israel Committee (May, 1983).

[7] The West German pollster, Elizabeth Noelle-Neuman, has termed "spiral of silence" the process by which a vocal minority opinion supplants a silent majority opinion. See her "The Spiral of Silence: a Theory of Public Opinion," *Journal of Communication* (1974), 43-51 and her "Return to the Concept of Powerful Mass Media" in H. Egushi, ed., *Studies of Broadcasting* (Tokyo: Nippon Hoso Kyokai, 1973).

[8] The League for Human Rights' national survey conducted in September, 1985 provides evidence that the Keegstra trial also contributed mainly to a climate of doubt rather than to a direct increase in anti-Jewish prejudice. Compared with responses to the League's 1984 survey, the September, 1985 survey showed that Canadians were as willing to vote for a Jewish candidate for office. Only fractionally more respondents said in September, 1985 than the previous year that Jews were too powerful. The major change in September, 1985 was how respondents perceived their neighbours. Far fewer thought that anti-Judaism was in decline in 1985 than had thought so the year before. When asked how media coverage of the Keegstra trial had affected public sentiment, more respondents declared seeing an increase in anti-Jewish feelings than a decrease. Our appreciation to Professor Taylor Buckner for this information.

Chapter 4

The Special Role of the Media

The Zundel trial was a media event. The main personality, the defendant, did what he could to capture media attention. His hard hat, his short controversial quotes, and his staged appearances were a recipe for camera exposure. He persuaded himself and many others that he was a master manipulator of the media. *Media Tactics I* and *Media Tactics II* were the titles of instructional audio tapes produced by the defendant and available for purchase during the course of the proceedings. Commentators and experts fell over themselves discussing how the media coverage would affect the Canadian public's beliefs about Nazism, the Holocaust, the justice system, and Jews. The trial received an exceptional volume of media attention.

The English-language big city media led in coverage of the affair. The English-language CBC's prime news period, 10-11 p.m.,[1] carried a total of 30 stories on Zundel from January 1st until the end of April with an almost daily diet in February. Toronto's *Globe and Mail,* Vancouver's *Sun,* and Calgary's *Herald* each provided their readers with 25 or more stories on the trial between January 1st and March 15th. The *Globe* provided the greatest exposure – 6 of its 31 stories appeared on page one. Radio Canada television did not provide as much coverage as CBC television but it did offer a total of 8 stories. During February, the Téléjournal and Le Point, counterparts of the National and Journal, gave their viewers one Zundel story every four days.

What effect should we expect this coverage to have had on the public mind? Two separate matters are at issue here – whether the media in democratic societies normally wield a powerful influence on public opinion, and whether Canadian journalists reported on the Zundel trial and the Holocaust in a responsible and noninjurious fashion. Our public opinion data can provide a partial answer to these questions.

Most of the commentators discussed in Chapter 1 said that heavy coverage of Zundel and his friends would lead to their being considered legitimate. *Saturday Night* editor Robert Fulford pointed to the headlines treating the Nazi witnesses at the trial as if they were objective researchers. Many commentators noted that Zundel was reported uncritically as if he were just another decent human being expressing the truth as he genuinely saw it.

CBC radio journalist Sandra Came told us that she and other journalists with whom she spoke were perfectly aware of how Zundel was seeking to manipulate the media, but felt obliged by journalistic ethics to report what he said as he said it without direct commentary.[2] John Owen, the Managing Editor of the CBC National TV News, told us that the Corporation's legal counsel insisted that Zundel's remarks be reported without interpretation in order to protect the integrity of the ongoing trial.[3]

Parallel to the debate among Canadians as to the responsibility of the press during the trial is a longstanding debate among communications scholars as to whether or not the media in liberal democratic societies are powerful molders of public opinion. According to those experts who view the media as powerful, the media set the agenda of public discussion and therefore decide what is important and what is unimportant.[4] Whether or not the media emphasize a particular issue affects the public's awareness of the issue. The media, it is said, construct reality by specifying which aspects or components of an issue or event merit reporting and which do not. Of special importance for our study is the view that the media confer special status or prestige on those who are highlighted in news reports or interviewed. For countless people, recognition by the media is evidence of a person's importance. Media power is circular. If you are truly important, you will be the focus of the public's attention. At the same time, if you are the focus of the public's attention, then you must really matter. The power of the media – particularly the power of television – becomes harmful in the case of those people who depend for their limited knowledge of the world on heavy exposure to the media. Studies of the impact of television on audiences show that heavy viewers often acquire quite erroneous views of the world in subject areas such as crime, ethnic groups, and even family life.[5] For example, television programming carries a high volume of violent programming and violent news with the result that heavy viewers exaggerate the degree of violence in the real world.

Many experts in mass communications take the view that the media are weak rather than strong molders of public opinion. Newspaper readers and television viewers do not after all have to believe or even absorb what they do not want to. Scholars have shown that people pay selective attention to and remember those facts which support what they always believed to be true. People can also test the validity of what they have learnt from the media by talking with their friends or by making analogies between the media message which they receive and their own personal observations and experiences.[6]

Our public opinion data can be used to help assess the validity of the two sides in the scholars' debate about media power and the two sides in the commentators' debate about responsible reporting during the Zundel trial. Altogether, four options are possible. Either the Canadian media were:

powerful and responsible,
powerful and irresponsible,
weak and responsible,
or weak and irresponsible.

Evidence from the public opinion data that exposure to the media strengthened anti-Jewish prejudice could be used to buttress the view that the media were powerful and acted irresponsibly. Evidence that media exposure reduced anti-Jewish prejudice could be used to support the view that the media were powerful and acted responsibly. Evidence of no change in the level of prejudice against Jews could be used to strengthen the view that the media were weak, whether or not they acted responsibly.

Canadians' Use of the Media

Our national survey asked respondents to report the extent to which they used television and the press. They were asked how many days a week they read news in a newspaper or watched news on television. Figs. 4.1 and 4.2 show that Canadians watch a lot of television and many read a daily newspaper. The majority (51%) reported watching television news every night. A large minority (38%) read newspapers every day. The average viewer saw television news 5 times a week while the average reader turned to his newspaper for news 4 times a week. A relatively large minority - one out of every five Canadians - did not read a newspaper at all.[7]

Fig 4.1

Number of Days Canadians Watch T.V. News Each Week

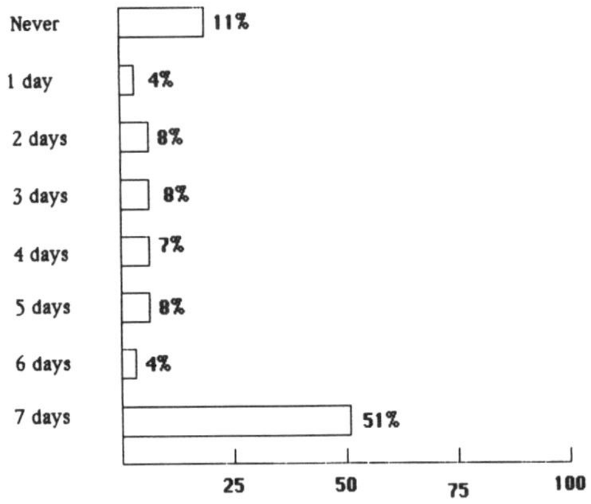

Number of Respondents 1047

Interpretation: Almost everyone watches T.V. News at least once a week. Half the population watches daily.

Fig 4.2

Number of Days Canadians Read a Newspaper Each week

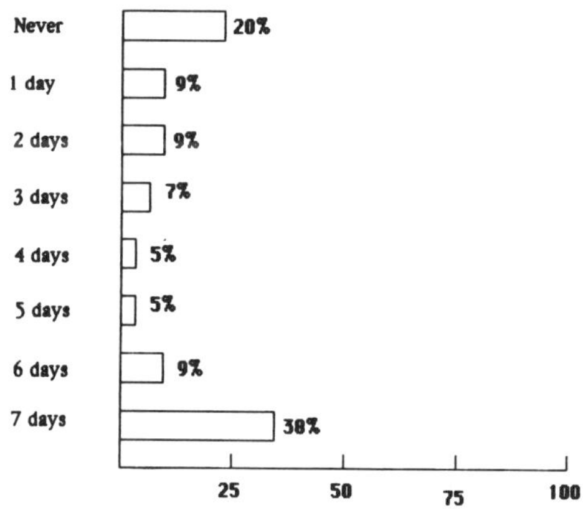

Number of Respondents 1045

Interpretation: Only 20% of Canadians do not read a paper while the largest group, 38%, read it every day

There was a modest tendency for people who read newspapers to watch television news and vice-versa.[8] Some people were more exposed to the press while others were more exposed to television. As found in many other studies of media use, those who relied heavily on television tended to have lower education and less prestigious jobs. Those who regularly read the daily newspaper were especially apt to be well educated. Since newspaper readers tend to be better educated than television viewers, we will examine individually the impact of each medium on public opinion.

Exposure to the Media and Awareness of the Trial

Our survey data confirmed the obvious, that the media played a major role in informing Canadians as a whole about the trial. The more people watched television news or read the paper, the more apt they were to know precisely why the defendant was charged. Those who were uninformed about the trial were mainly those who were never exposed to either medium. The proportion of Canadians who were oblivious to the trial was only 38% among daily TV watchers and as high as 69% among those who watched only once a week. The proportion who were oblivious to the trial was only 37% among those who read a paper each day and as high as 69% among those who never read a paper (figs. 4.3 and 4.4.).

Of course, one may argue that the reason why media users – especially newspaper readers – were better informed is that they were better educated. Better educated people are normally better informed. In order to keep themselves informed, educated people make certain that they read the press and watch television news. Hence, according to this line of argument, education rather than the media was the true cause of an informed public. There is certainly some truth to this argument, but how much truth is the question.

If education *contributed* to an informed public, we should expect better educated people to have been better informed. We showed above that this was true in the case of the Zundel trial. If education were *the sole cause* of an informed public, we should expect that exposure to the media did *not* contribute to more knowledge of the trial *within each* level of education. Examining only the responses of people with low education (elementary school), we should find that heavy media users were no more informed than light media users if the media did not in fact help inform the public. We should likewise find that media use and knowledge of the trial were unrelated in the case of people with medium education (high school) and in the case of people with high education (university).

Fig 4.3

T.V. Exposure and Knowledge of the Trial

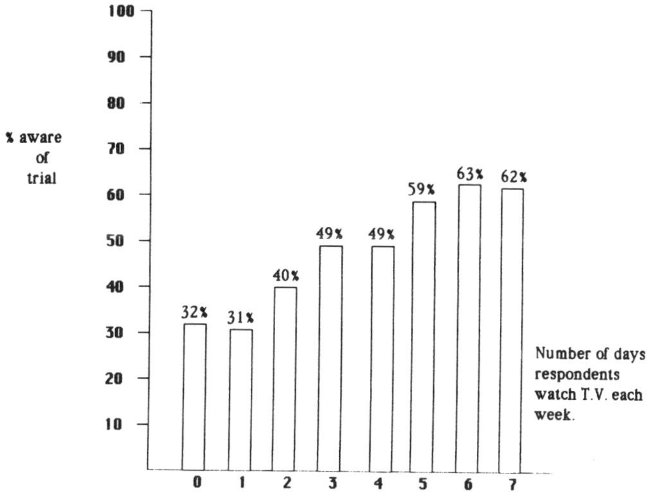

Interpretation : The more people watched T.V. news, the more they became knowledgeable of the trial.

Fig 4.4

Newspaper Use and Knowledge of the Trial

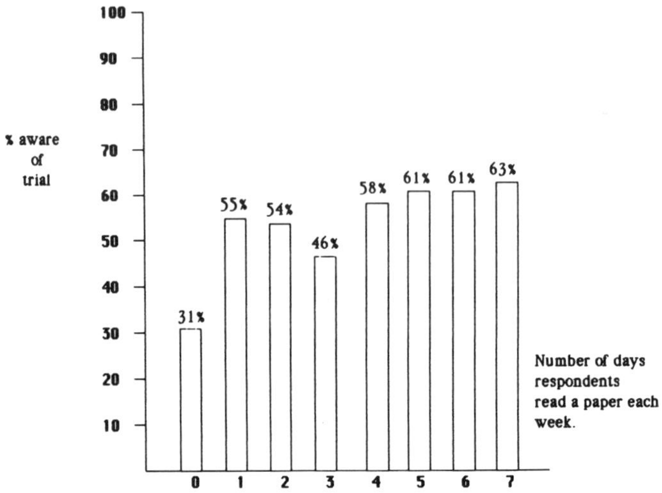

Interpretation: The more people used the press, the more they tended to become knowledgeable of the trial.

Fig 4.5

The Impact of Media Exposure on Knowledge of the Trial for People of Low, Medium and High Education.

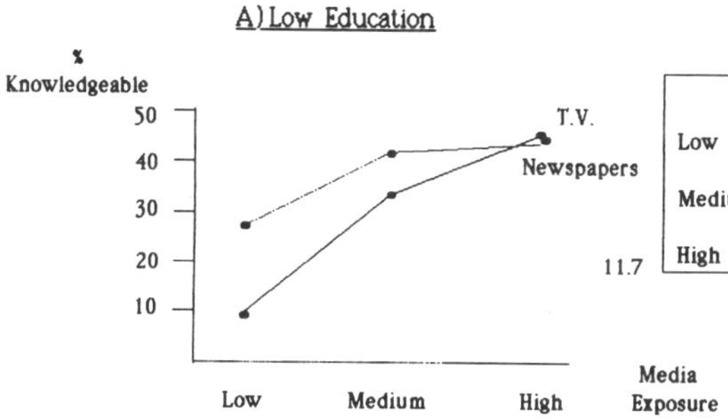

In %

	T.V.	Newspaper
Low	12	28
Medium	37	42
High	45	44

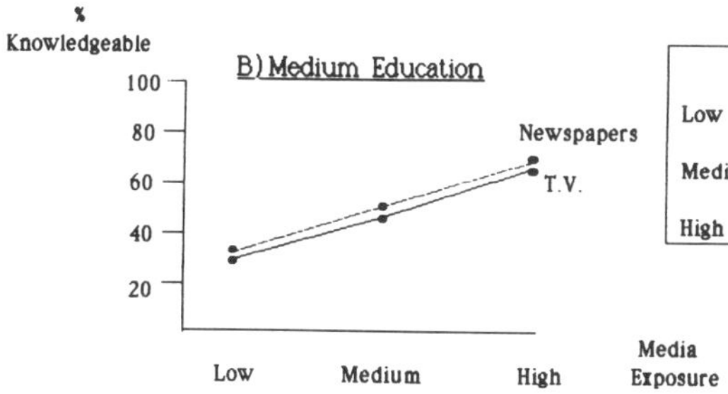

In %

	T.V.	Newspaper
Low	32	35
Medium	50	54
High	65	68

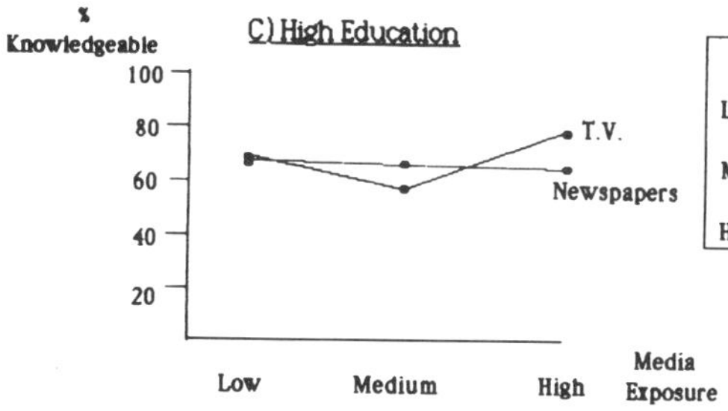

In %

	T.V.	Newspaper
Low	70	70
Medium	54	68
High	77	67

Interpretation: Media exposure increased knowledge of the trial among people with low and medium education, but not high education.

Fig 4.6

T.V. Exposure and Increased Sympathy for Jews.

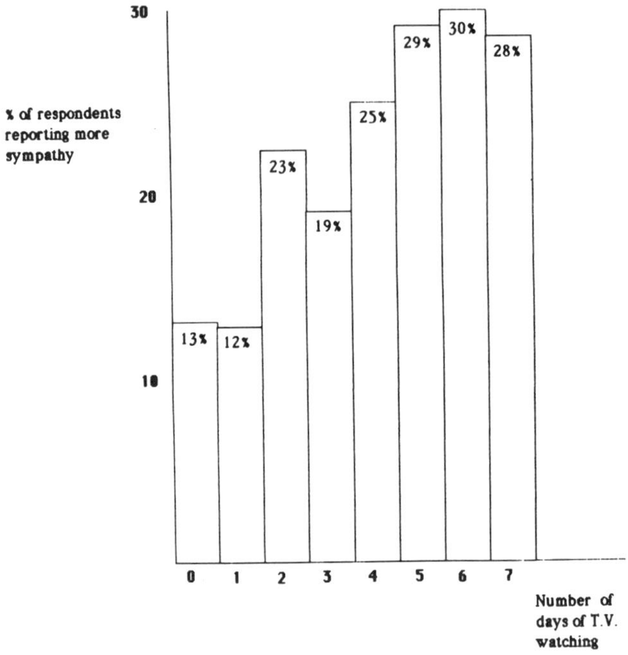

Interpretation: Heavy T.V. watchers were more likely to say that their sympathy for Jews increased as a result of the trial.

Fig. 4.5 contains information from the survey which helps us decide whether education alone or education plus the media caused Canadians to be informed of the trial. The figure contains three parts – one part each for Canadians of low, medium, and high education. The lines within each of the three graphs show whether increased use of television and the press produced increased knowledge of the trial. If the media helped inform the public, the lines should rise; otherwise, they should remain flat (horizontal) or even perhaps decline.

Our data shows that the media contributed significantly to knowledge of the trial among people with low and medium education, but not among those with high education. Highly educated people may have learnt about the issue from their friends or even from the media, but they did not need repeated exposure to learn the issues. For people with low and medium education, the more they normally used the media, the better informed they became as a result. University graduates were highly informed about the issue almost irrespective of how much of little they used the media. Among university graduates, 70% or light TV watchers understood the charge against Zundel as compared to 78% among heavy viewers. High school graduates reached the same level of understanding as university graduates if they became heavy media users, reading a paper or watching TV news 6 or 7 times a week.[9] The number of high school graduates who understood the issue was more than twice as high among heavy media users as among light.

The study of the Eichmann trial also found that the media played a role in informing the public. Those Americans who were most knowledgeable about the Eichmann trial were more likely to report learning about the issue from the mass media. Exposure to the media explained knowledge of the Eichmann case to the same degree as media exposure in Canada explained knowledge of the Zundel case. In our Canadian study, those respondents who were exposed to neither medium were profoundly ill-informed. As many as 92% of this small group did not know about the case, the highest level of ignorance found by any factor used in this study.

The role of the media was different in the Eichmann and Zundel cases in one respect. In the American study, the printed word was the more efficient source of information. In the Canadian case, both media served to inform the public with equal efficiency. This difference may be explained by the changed role of television from the 1960's to the present time. Television has become a more important part of daily life and the production of television news, a more serious business, especially perhaps in Canada.

The Media and Changed Sympathies

The next question to explore is how the media affected the public's sympathies for Jews and Germans. Focussing on those who knew what the trial was about, we compared the degree of exposure to the media with respondents' changed sympathies. Tables 4.1 and 4.2 contain information on the relationship between media use and sympathy for Jews and Germans in a detailed quantitative format for readers who enjoy reading numbers. Readers who do not like to read numbers can turn to fig. 4.6, which shows in graphical form the impact of media exposure on attitudes toward Jews.

Fig. 4.6 and table 4.1 demonstrate that TV viewing and sympathy for Jews are strongly related. The proportion of people who reported becoming more sympathetic to Jews rose consistently as Canadians watched more television news. The proportion becoming more sympathetic to Jews rose from 12% among light viewers (0-1 day per week) to as high as 29% among heavy viewers (6-7 days). Moreover, exposure to television dramatically lowered the number of respondents who said that they did not know how their feelings were affected by the trial – from 46% among non-viewers to 21% among heavy viewers. Heavy exposure to television news led to a clearer perception of how one's feelings changed and a more sympathetic view of Jews. *Exposure to television contributed to positive feelings towards Jews.*

A different picture emerges when sympathy towards Germans is analysed. The main effect of heavy TV viewing is to maintain pre-existing levels of sympathy for Germans. The higher the exposure to television, the more people claim that their sympathy for Germans remained unchanged. The proportions of people who changed their feelings about Germans – who became either more sympathetic or less sympathetic – did not vary according to level of television use. In the case of attitudes to Germans, television exposure reinforced existing feelings and reduced the level of uncertainty about these feelings were. Altogether, television played a very different role in affecting sympathies towards Jews and Germans.

What was the role of the press in shaping sympathies? Table 4.2 shows that the press also increased sympathies for Jews but not at all to the same degree. Non-readers were less apt to become sympathetic to Jews than readers. But, heavy readers were no more likely to become sympathetic than light readers. The main effect of the press was to reduce the number of people who do not know how their feelings towards Jews were affected. The proportion who do not know how their sympathy for Jews was affected by the trial dropped sharply from 44% among nonreaders to 21% among daily readers. Newspaper reading also increased the number of people who said

Table 4.1
T.V. Exposure and Change of Sympathy
(in percent) towards Jews/Germans

No. of Days Per Week Watching T.V.	Towards Jews				Towards Germans			
	More Sympathetic	Less Sympathetic	The Same	Don't Know	More Sympathetic	Less Sympathetic	The Same	Don't Know
0	13	2	40	46	4	12	38	46
1	12	2	43	43	2	12	41	45
2	23	0	46	32	0	13	53	34
3	19	3	53	26	4	12	54	31
4	25	3	43	29	6	19	43	32
5	29	4	45	22	2	15	54	29
6	30	2	46	22	4	18	58	20
7	28	2	49	21	4	13	61	22

Table 4.2
Newspaper Readership and Change of Sympathy Towards Jews/Germans

No. of Days Per Week Reading Newspaper	Towards Jews				Towards Germans			
	More Sympathetic	Less Sympathetic	The Same	Don't Know	More Sympathetic	Less Sympathetic	The Same	Don't Know
0	17	2	37	44	3	12	40	44
1	26	3	41	30	3	15	50	32
2	21	5	53	21	5	14	56	26
3	25	3	50	22	3	16	57	24
4	28	0	50	22	4	20	48	28
5	31	2	48	19	2	12	65	22
6	25	1	54	20	2	15	61	23
7	27	2	50	21	5	12	61	23

that their feelings about Jews remained the same as before. As in the case of television, the press did not affect the number of people who were either friendly or unfriendly towards Germans. As in the case of the consumption of television news, exposure to newspapers dramatically reduced the number of people who were unsure of their feelings towards Germans while increasing the number of people who said that their feelings remained the same as before.

The relationship between media exposure and changed sympathies is complex. TV viewing led to more sympathy for Jews as a result of the trial and to no change in sympathy for Germans. Newspaper reading led mainly to increased numbers of people saying that their feelings were unaffected by the case. These different impacts can be explained partly by differences in the markets served by the two media. Heavy newspaper readers are well educated, well informed, and have relatively well developed opinions. They are apt to have background information on any given topic, often drawn from years of reading books and periodicals or viewing special documentaries and public affairs programs on television. Because they are well informed, heavy newspaper readers depend less on the press for their knowledge and evaluation of the world around them. By contrast, heavy television users are less well educated, less well informed, and therefore more susceptible to the messages which they absorb from the medium. They are less likely to have a wealth of previous information from which to evaluate what they see on television and they are less likely to face television news reporting with an already developed opinion.

The greater impact of television may also be explained by the nature of the medium. Television is said to be a "hot" medium as contrasted with the "cool," rational printed word.[10] The television coverage included some shocking film footage and eye witness testimonies on the death camps, mass burial, gas chambers, train loads of corpses and other evocative material. The greater emotional potential of television and its less informed audience combine to explain its greater impact on public opinion.

The Media and Attitudes about the Holocaust

The media played an important role in creating knowledge of the trial and in molding sympathies. Did the media also affect how the public received Zundel's messages about the Holocaust? Could the public have become more sympathetic to Jews while at the same time accepting some of Zundel's assertions about the Holocaust? In view of the status conferred on Zundel by the media, could some of his views of the Holocaust have found receptive ears?

To analyse the potential effect of media coverage, we examined the respondents' answers to questions about the existence of the Holocaust, responsibility for the victimization of Jews, and the power of Jews. We compared their answers according to how much television news they watched and how often they read newspapers.

For low, medium, and high TV and newspaper users, Table 4.3 displays the survey responses to the question about whether six million died, to the question about whether Jews were to blame, and to the question about whether more people now doubt the historical record of the period. *The table shows a discernible increase in the frequency of non-hostile answers for each level of media use.* The more they consumed information from the press or television a medium of communication, the more respondents were apt to accept the six million estimate as true, to hold Jews blameless for their victimization, and to believe that no one questions the record of that period of history. For example, 43% of low television users agreed that the six million estimate was about right as compared to 48% among medium viewers and 54% among high viewers. Similarly, 46% of low newspaper readers accepted the estimate as compared to 48% of medium readers and 56% of high newspaper readers.

Televison exercised a particularly strong influence on whether people thought that their fellow citizens now doubted the record of the Holocaust. The proportion of people who believe that "almost no one" now doubts the record of the period rose from 16% among low television users to 27% among high users. Television had no impact on whom people held responsible for the atrocities. Heavy viewers were no more likely to hold Jews faultless than light viewers. The failure of television to influence whom people blamed for the Holocaust may be explained partly by the fact that most people already knew whom to blame. Three out of five Canadians held Jews faultless as compared to one out of two who believed that six million had perished and only one out of five who thought that "almost no one" now questioned the record of that period in history. Whereas many people said that they were not sure how many people perished or how many people now doubted the historical record of the period, very few people were unsure of whom to hold responsible. Another reason television may have failed to influence whom its audience blamed is that the time and format limitations of television make it difficult for the medium to explain why events occur. Still another reason why increased exposure to television did not affect whom the audience blamed is that the television audience is less educated and hence less capable of analytic thinking than the readership of newspapers.

To this point, we have looked at the impact of television and the press on Canadians as a whole. In chapters 2 and 3, we showed that English and French Canada were different. French-speaking Canadians were less apt to

Table 4.3
Media Use and Holocaust Related Attitudes

	Six Million		Jews' Fault		Questioning the Record	
	About Right	Don't Know	Not Jews' Fault	Don't Know	About No One	Don't Know
T.V.						
Low	43	34	58	27	16	53
Medium	48	32	61	23	19	34
High	54	23	61	20	28	27
Newspaper						
Low	46	29	56	28	21	43
Medium	48	21	59	21	20	30
High	56	19	64	19	26	29

be informed of the trial and less apt to become sympathetic to Jews. What role did the media play in influencing English and French Canadians?

The English and French media exercised similar impacts on awareness of the trial among the two language groups. In both English and French Canada, knowledge of the trial grew substantially as people watched television or read the newspaper more frequently (see fig. 4.7). The basic difference between the English and French media effects is that English Canadians were more widely informed about the trial at each level of media use. Among anglophones watching television at most once a week, as many as 43% knew what the trial was about. Among the corresponding group of French-speaking abstainers from TV, not a single respondent – 0% – knew what the trial was about. In the case of English Canadians, the proportion who were informed of the trial rose from 43% among low TV viewers to 67% among high TV viewers. In the case of French Canadians, it grew from 0% to 36%. The basic reason why French Canadians who do not watch much television or rarely read a newspaper knew little about the trial is that the French media gave little coverage to it. French Canadians had to use their media more often to get the same volume of information. We shall return to a discussion of media coverage in a moment.

The English and French media influenced the sympathies of their audiences but in slightly different ways. In both communities, high television viewers were more apt to say that their sympathies for Jews had grown as a result of the trial (fig. 4.8). In both communities, exposure to television doubled the number of people expressing greater sympathy for Jews. Comparing light and heavy viewers, the proportions expressing greater sympathy for Jews were 17% and 32% among anglophones and 7% and 17% among francophones.

Yet, television viewing did not have exactly the same effect among anglophones and francophones. *For English Canadians, the principal effect of television was to increase sympathy for Jews but for French Canadians this was a secondary effect. Among French Canadians, the principal change was a dramatic decline in the proportion who said that they did not know how they felt and a dramatic increase in the number who said that they experienced no change in sympathy.* Among French speakers, the number of people saying that they did not know how their feelings had changed was halved as a result of television exposure – from 79% to 39%. Meanwhile, the number of French Canadians reporting no change in their feelings increased three-fold – from 14% to 43%.

Heavy anglophone and francophone viewers are a study in contrasts. Among English Canadians who watched a lot of television news, a significant minority became more sympathetic to Jews – almost a third. Not so in

Fig 4.7

T.V. Exposure and knowledge of the Trial by Language

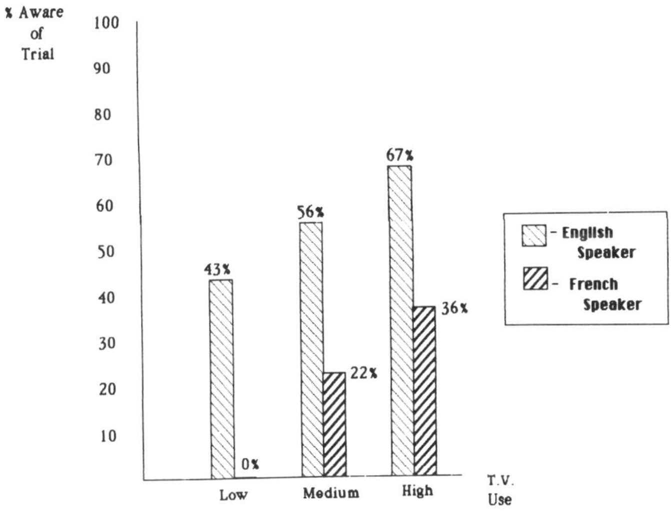

Interpretation: Knowledge of the trial increased as a result of exposure to television among both anglophones and francophones.

Fig 4.8

T.V. Exposure and Increased Sympathy - English vs. French

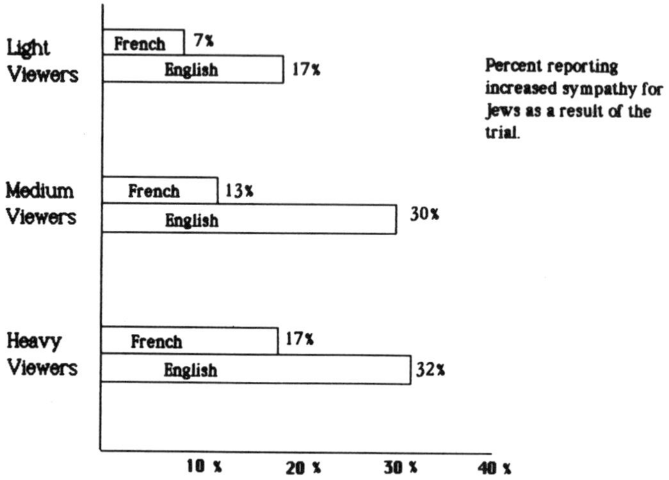

Interpretation: T.V. exposure strengthened sympathy in each community. The level of sympathy was always higher among the anglophones.

French Canada. The effect of exposure to the French media was partly to augment sympathy, but mainly to solidify previous feelings among francophones. When French-speaking respondents reported that the trial made them feel about Jews the way they had always felt, it is safe to assume that their traditional feelings were neutral or negative rather than positive. Many scholars from different disciplines have written about the strain of anti-Judaism in Quebec nationalism, a tendency which they often attributed to the influence of Roman Catholic theology.[11]

The media effects in English and French Canada differ in another respect as well. In English Canada, exposure to television or the press increased knowledge of the trial among people with low and medium education but not among the highly educated. Highly educated anglophones were informed about the trial whether or not they were heavy consumers of the media. In French Canada, media exposure increased knowledge among people with medium and high education but not among those with low education. Poorly educated francophones – a group in society highly prejudiced against Jews – remained oblivious to the trial whether or not they were exposed to the media.

Explaining the Impact of the Media

The commentators discussed in Chapter 1 provided some arguments that Zundel manipulated the Canadian media and that his and his witnesses' wild assertions were treated by journalists as if they were normal opinions or facts. Readers will remember that the tragic fact of crematoria became, in the context of the trial, a mere "theory." Zundel boasted of his publicity coups. CBC News, the *Globe and Mail,* and other media outlets received complaints about biased coverage from interested Christians, from Jews, and even from worried journalists themselves. Many journalists were deeply concerned. The CBC National news staff held many meetings to review their coverage during the course of the trial and to discuss how to be fair. Given the commentators' concern that Zundel was outwitting the media, how can we explain the unforeseen, benign impact of the English media and the mixed effect of the French media?

It is true that the media reports on the trial often bent over backwards to report Zundel's perspective in an apparently dispassionate way. A *Globe and Mail* headline read "No gas chambers in Nazi Germany, expert witness testifies." Since the witness was France's convicted hatemonger, Robert Faurisson, the headline could just as easily have been "No gas chambers in Germany, says Nazi apologist." However, it needs to be remembered that the media also covered the legal case of the Crown. CBC television and most

English language dailies reported the testimonies of Holocaust survivors and of distinguished, expert witnesses. A story on the testimony of one survivor began as follows:

> "An escaper from Auschwitz concentration camp told a Toronto court yesterday of having to roam through cattle cars of weeping Jews in search of the dead, the injured."[12]

The witness was University of British Columbia Professor Rudolf Vrba. He and other survivors as well as expert witnesses were featured on prime time television and in newspaper coverage of the trial.

Just as important as the coverage given to Crown witnesses at the trial was the media's extensive coverage of events which were not related in a legal sense to the trial but which might well have influenced how the public viewed the trial. Holocaust stories unrelated to the trial received extensive coverage in the media, especially the English media. One such story was the 40th anniversary of the liberation of the annihilation camps and the reunion in Jerusalem of survivors, including twins upon whom Dr. Joseph Mengele had conducted gruesome experiments. During the January 1st - March 15th period, the *Globe and Mail* provided 23 stories on the Holocaust as compared to 31 on the Zundel trial. During the corresponding January - March period in the 1984, a year earlier, the paper provided a total of 16 stories on the Holocaust and none on Zundel. Thus, the *Globe* provided its readers with a substantial volume of information from which to judge what actually happened during the horrific period. Other newspapers provided the same breadth of service. For example, during the January 1st - March 15th, 1985 period, the *Calgary Herald* carried 27 stories on the trial and as many as 42 on the events of the Holocaust. The *Herald's* intensive coverage may have been prompted by the events in neighbouring Eckville. Newfoundland's *Evening Standard* carried 12 stories on Zundel and as many as 27 on the Holocaust.

CBC television news also provided its audience with information helpful in understanding European history. During the actual period of the trial, January - March, 1985, the National and Journal focussed on the trial itself. The trial received more than five times more coverage than the Holocaust, 78 minutes, 10 seconds of coverage as compared to 12 mins., 54 secs.[13] But, over the 17 month period beginning in January, 1984, the Holocaust received considerably more attention than the trial or its defendant. Of the 221 prime time minutes devoted to the two subjects, 61% went to the Holocaust. In January, 1984, the Journal carried a special two part series on the role of France's Vichy government in the "final solution." In May, 1984, the National carried a story on a reunion of Holocaust survivors. In January, 1985, the National carried stories on Swedish Holocaust hero Raoul Wallenberg and the 40th anniversary of the liberation of Auschwitz.

During the January - March, 1985 period of the trial, the French language Radio Canada television network actually gave more coverage to the Holocaust than to the trial. Radio-Canada carried repeated stories on the death camps' macabre experimenter, Dr. Mengele, whose grave was unearthed in South America.

To summarize to this point, the media balanced their apparently neutral reporting of Holocaust denial with significant exposure for Holocaust survivors testifying at the trial and with very extensive reporting on the Holocaust outside the context of the trial. Media users had good opportunities to learn the facts of the Holocaust outside the context of the trial itself. Viewers of television and readers of the press could decide for themselves if the Holocaust had ever taken place.

Of course, Zundel's case was not limited to saying that the Holocaust was a fraud which never took place. He asserted that Jews are a satanic people who fabricated the myth of the Holocaust to enhance their ability to exploit the world. Even if convinced that the annihilation camps did exist, ordinary Canadians might nonetheless have been persuaded that Jews were somehow responsible for the unfolding of events. Canadians might have been especially susceptible to unfriendly feelings if they knew little about Jewish life and if their limited information about Judaism came from unfriendly religious or secular sources. What the media said about Jewish life outside the framework of Zundel or the Holocaust might have a bearing on how the public responds. Jews in the context of Zundel and the Holocaust are essentially impersonal victims in history with limited individual identity. It is difficult for people to identify emotionally with impersonal victims in history. Even objective media reporting on the Holocaust may not lessen anti-Jewish prejudice. From the fact that Jews were victimized, poorly informed people might conclude that Jews must have done something to cause it. A historic view held by some Christians even today is that the oppression of the Jews is evidence of God's wrath over their rejection of Jesus.[14] The media may be able to reduce anti-Jewish prejudice by conveying information on ordinary Jewish life today. News reports on ordinary Jewish life permit Jews to be portrayed as individuals, with their own dreams, achievements, and shortcomings.

The media West of Quebec generally provided considerable reporting on Jewish affairs. In the January-March, 1985 period, the *Globe* carried 14 nonviolent Jewish stories and 6 pictures as compared to 23 Holocaust stories and 3 pictures. The Vancouver *Sun* carried 16 nonviolent Jewish stories as compared to 17 on the Holocaust. The *Calgary Herald* carried 7 nonviolent Jewish stories. Over the 17 month period beginning in January, 1984, CBC-TV's National and Journal devoted 63 minutes to nonviolent Jewish events as compared to 85 minutes on the trial and 135 minutes on the Holocaust. In September, 1984 the National carried a story on a new female rabbi. In November, the National reported on the Ethiopian Jews while the Journal carried a special report on the prize-winning Yiddish novelist, I.B. Singer. In January, 1985, the Journal's arts section carried a Jewish segment.

The media in Quebec and Newfoundland differed from the media elsewhere in their treatment of the trial, the Holocaust, and especially Jewish events. Readers will recall that French Quebecers and Newfoundlanders were especially apt to be unaware of the trial and to adopt unsympathetic views while people in Ontario, Saskatchewan, and British Columbia were most apt to be informed and sympathetic. We compared the content of Radio-Canada, Montreal's *La Presse,* Quebec City's *Le Soleil,* and Newfoundland's *Evening Telegram* on the one hand with the CBC, the *Globe,* the Vancouver *Sun,* and to a lesser extent, the Calgary *Herald.* Interestingly, the members of the latter group provided much more coverage of both the trial and the Holocaust. But, the biggest difference is that the media in the regions of the country with smaller anti-Jewish minorities provided considerable coverage of non-violent Jewish issues while the media in the regions with larger anti-Jewish minorities provided virtually no such coverage at all. The *Globe* and *Sun* averaged 15 non-violent Jewish stories during the period of the trial. The Calgary *Herald* carried 7. The two French papers and the Newfoundland paper carried not one. During the July, 1984 - May, 1985 period, the CBC carried ten times more coverage of non-violent Jewish stories than Radio-Canada, 39 minutes vs. 4 minutes. Radio-Canada's entire non-violent Jewish coverage was devoted to the fleeing Ethiopian Jews, providing another theme of victimization. French-speaking Canadians have little opportunity to learn from their media about Jews other than in a context of persecution. The absence of nonviolent Jewish content on the French media poses a problem because French Canadians, as Chapter 6 will show, have the least contact with Jews and are also the least sympathetic.

The journalists at Radio-Canada, *La Presse, Le Soleil,* and the *Evening Telegram* face a catch-22 situation. The absence of nonviolent Jewish content and the relative lack of Holocaust content may reflect the preferences of their audiences. On the other hand, a changed reportorial menu would do some good for inter-group relations. Increased French language television coverage of the Holocaust and especially nonviolent Jewish events may be particularly effective for reaching francophones of low education.

The last remaining question to consider is whether the heavy coverage of the Holocaust and of nonviolent Jewish events in the English media resulted from the conscious decisions of journalists seeking to neutralize Zundel's impact or whether these events received a normal level of attention. Did

English Canadian journalists purposefully increase their coverage of the Holocaust and of nonviolent Jewish events in order to balance the macabre coverage of the Zundel trial? Or, were there simply more newsworthy Holocaust and Jewish events to be reported? Some of the journalists with whom we spoke said that they purposefully increased the Holocaust coverage. Some journalists may have increased Holocaust or nonviolent Jewish coverage on purpose while others may have done so without conscious thought. Our research does not provide a clear answer.

We compared the volume of coverage of the Zundel trial, the Holocaust, and nonviolent Jewish themes in various Canadian media and in three British and American newspapers for two periods, January - March, 1984 and January - March, 1985. First, we compared 1984 and 1985 coverage in English Canada. Our results were mixed. The CBC's coverage of the Holocaust and nonviolent Jewish events did not rise in 1985, but the *Globe's* did. At the *Globe,* Holocaust stories increased from 13 to 19 while nonviolent Jewish stories increased from 3 to 14. Secondly, we wanted to see if the volume of such stories increased from 1984 to 1985 in the *New York Times,* the *Times* of London, and the *Guardian*. If the foreign papers kept their coverage at a constant level, the *Globe's* increase might be attributed to journalistic decisions. But, our foreign results were mixed as well. Coverage increased at the *Times* of London but not at the *Guardian* and not at the *New York Times*. *Our conclusion is that some Canadian journalists and perhaps some Canadian media may have augmented their coverage of the Holocaust and nonviolent Jewish events to neutralize Zundel's impact, but the English Canadian did not do so as a whole.*

* * * * *

Our survey data show that Canadians are heavy consumers of the mass media and that the media make an important difference. Viewers of television and readers of newspapers are more apt to know about the trial – particularly in the case of anglophones with low or medium education and francophones with medium or high education. Heavy media exposure enabled high school graduates to acquire the same understanding of the issue as university graduated with low or medium exposure.

Media exposure – especially exposure to television – increased sympathy for Jews. Exposure to the media also increased the public's knowledge of the Holocaust and reduced the frequency with which respondents expressed hostile Holocaust-related attitudes towards Jews. Media exposure did not reduce the frequency with which Jews were said to have too much power. Altogether, media exposure increased understanding of the Holocaust among those Canadians who were not hostile at the outset while failing to reduce the size of the prejudiced minority.

Media impacts were different in English and French Canada. The main impact of media exposure in English Canada was to augment sympathy for Jews while this was a secondary impact in French Canada. The main impact of exposure on francophones was to reinforce longstanding feelings. The different impacts in English and French Canada were attributed in part to different treatments by the media of Jewish issues. The English media not only provided greater trial coverage, but also greater Holocaust coverage and the only coverage of nonviolent Jewish events. French Canadians had very little opportunity to learn from the media about ordinary Jewish life outside a context of victimization.

The chapter began by considering two questions – whether or not the media in democratic societies are powerful or weak molders of public opinion and whether Canadian reporting of the Zundel affair was responsible.

Our public opinion data suggest that the media were moderately powerful and behaved in a responsible fashion. The fact that heavy consumers of television and press news did not become more anti-Jewish inspite of the publicity for Zundel suggests that the media generally acted in a constructive and noninjurous fashion. The fact that increased exposure to TV news was associated with increased sympathy for Jews suggests that television broadcasters behaved in a responsible way and also exercised some degree of power or influence over the formation of public opinion.

It is unfortunate that the trial engendered some degree of anti-German feeling among the Canadian public. Anti-German feeling might have been mitigated had more German Canadians spoken out against Zundel and had the media given greater coverage to those who did.

We are not saying that all media reports on the proceedings of the trial were satisfactory. Our goal was not to enter into a debate about the quality of courtroom reports in any particular newspaper or on any particular day. *Saturday Night* editor Rober t Fulford and other commentators may have been correct to criticize specific headlines or story contents in particular newspapers. Our evidence merely allow us to conclude that the overall effect of exposure to television news and/or the press was noninjurious and, in some instances, beneficial.

[1] The Toronto-based English network of the CBC provides the "National" news program at 10 p.m. followed by the "Journal" public affairs program lasting until 11 p.m. The corresponding shows for the Montreal-based French language Radio-Canada are the "Telejournal" and "Le Point."

[2] Personal communication to Gabriel Weimann, Spring, 1985.

[3] Personal communication to Conrad Winn, Spring, 1985.

[4] For a classic statement of the view that the media are powerful molders of public opinion, see Elizabeth Noelle-Neumann, "Return to the Concept of the Powerful Mass Media" in H. Equchi and K. Sata, eds., *Studies of Broadcasting* (1973), 67-112. For an important overview of the evidence of media influence on society, see Elihu Katz, "On Conceptualizing Media Effects" in T. McCormack, ed., *Mass Media: Decade of Dissent* (Greenwich, Conn.: JAI Press, 1980).

[5] G. Gerbner, L. Gross, M. Morgan, and N. Signorielli, "The 'Mainstreaming' of America, Violence Profil No. 11," *Journal of Communication* (1980), 10-29.

[6] J. Klapper, *The Effects of Mass Communication* (New York: Free Press, 1950).

[7] About 4% of the sample interviewed said that they were exposed to neither television nor the press. These non-users of the media tended to be old people, Quebecers, Roman Catholics, urban dwellers, and females.

[8] Statistically minded readers may note that the product-moment correlation between use of press and television news was a statistically significant but modest +0.29.

[9] Light media users were those who read or watched 0-1 day per week; medium users, 2-5 days; heavy users, 6-7 days.

[10] See "Media Hot and Cold" in Marshall McLuhan, *Understanding Media* (Toronto: McGraw Hill, 1965).

[11] Horace Minor, *St. Denis* (Chicago: University of Chicago Press, 1939), E.C. Hughes, *French Canada in Transition* (Chicago: University of Chicago Press, 1943), A.J. Belanger, *L'Apolitisme des Ideologies Québecoises* (Ste. Foy: Les Presses de l'Université Laval, 1974), F. Dumont *et al.*, *Idéologies au Canada Francais, 1900-1929* (Ste. Foy: Les Presses de l'Université Laval, 1973), R. Jones, *L'Idéologie de l'Action Catholique* (Ste. Foy: Les Presses de l'Université Laval, 1973), Lita-Rose Betcherman, *The Swastika and the Maple Leaf* (Toronto: Fitzhenry and Whiteside, 1975), and Victor Téboul, *Mythe et Images du Juif au Quebec* (Montreal: Editions de Lagrave, 1978). For a survey-based study, see Werner Cohn. "English and French Canadian Public Opinion on Jews and Israel: Some Poll Data," *Canadian Ethnic Studies* (1979), 31-48. For a marxist study which seeks to explain Quebec's anti-Jewish strain in terms of the economic subordination of the French by the English and anti-English animosity misdirected towards the Jews, see Denis Monière, *Le Développement des Idéologies au Québec* (Montreal: Editions Quebec/Amérique, 1977).

[12] Kirk Makin, "Escaper tells of arrivals at Auschwitz," Globe and Mail, January 22nd, 1985.

[13] All data on the reporting of the English language CBC are made possible thanks to the generosity of John Owen, Managing Editor, National TV News, and Laura

Marshall. The data for the French language Radio Canada network are made possible thanks to the generosity of André Bouchard, Assistant Editor-in-chief, television news.

14 In the period before World War II, the leading Protestant journal, *Christian Century,* wrote that it did not want to encourage "aggressive Jews to claim the country [of Palestine] as a 'homeland' for their people." Jewish nationalism was ominous because "it was nationalism among the Jews that crucified Jesus." The journal proceeded to admit candidly that "the Christian mind has never allowed itself to feel the same human concern for Jewish sufferings that it has felt for the cruelties visited upon [others] . . . Christian indifference to Jewish sufferings has for centuries been rationalized by *the tenable belief that such sufferings were the judgment of God upon the Jewish people for their rejection of Jesus.*" (emphasis added). Peter Grose, *Israel in the Mind of America* (New York: Alfred A. Knopf, 1984), 96-97. The idea that the Jew is condemned to wander the earth in perpetual misery as punishment for rejecting Jesus is expressed clearly in a text which was an authorized school book in New Brunswick until 1985. See *Les Plus Belles Légendes Acadiennes* (Montreal: Stanké, 1983).

Chapter 5

Prejudice and Ignorance

Our book has shown that the trial neither created nor intensified anti-Judaism. In English Canada in particular, the mass media's portrayal of the trial and other related issues produced a modest educational effect. Within French Canada, the trial yielded both positive and nonpositive effects. However, the nonpositive effect in French Canada – a reinforcement of prior attitudes towards Jews – cannot be credited to Zundel since he was not interested in French Canada and made little effort to make his case there.[1] Within English Canada, one of several reasons for Zundel's failure is that he did not reach those people of low education and low media use who would be most receptive to his arguments if only he managed to reach them. Holocaust denial existed in Canada before Holocaust "revisionists" made their appearance. Given that Zundel did not create anti-Judaism in Canada, the tasks are to assess the magnitude of the problem and to identify its sources. These are the tasks of Chapters 5 and 6.

Social scientists studying animosity between groups have traditionally focussed on whether the members of groups know each other and have friendships across group lines. Animosity often goes together with isolation. An effective way of finding out if Canadians have contact with Jews and how they feel about Jews is to ask them. The best way of asking Canadians about Jews is by asking them about other ethnic groups at the same time. Asking respondents about several groups avoids singling out in their minds any particular group. Furthermore, asking about several groups can help give meaning to people's views about any particular group.

National surveys were conducted in 1983 and 1984 asking Canadians about their relations with and feelings about several different ethnic groups. We repeated these questions in 1985, at the end of the trial. To find out if Canadians have met or personally know members of various ethnic groups, we asked the following question: *"Do you have contact with any member of these ethnic groups – often, occasionally, rarely, never?"* The 1983 and 1984 surveys asked about Jews, Italians, and Poles.[2] Our 1985 survey asked about Jews, Italians, Blacks, Asians, Germans, and Scots. In the Canadian context, Blacks and Asians are obvious outgroups. The many "Situation Reports" commissioned by the Multiculturalism Directorate of the federal government have provided considerable evidence of discrimination and violence against members of these groups. There also exists convincing proof of discrimination in employment against Blacks seeking advertised jobs.[3] Germans were included among the list of ethnic groups because of the German theme repeatedly raised by the defendant in the trial and of course because of the Holocaust. Scots were included as the paramount example of a top-dog group. Almost since the Conquest of New France, Canadians of Anglo-Scottish origin have occupied a special place in the corporate boardrooms and higher civil service of the nation.

Table 5.1 shows that the pattern of contact with Jews remained the same over the three year period and that as many as two out of five Canadians are not aware of having made contact with a Jew. Given that contact between groups may reduce mistrust, the fact that approximately 40% of Canadians reported no contact ever may be an alarming figure. Our respondents said that they were more apt to have relations with members of every other group except Asians (see table 5.2). In 1985, the number of Canadians who said that they had no contact ever with Jews was 43% as it was also in the case of Asians. The 43% rate for Jews compared with 34% in the case of Germans. The fact that two out of five Canadians have never knowingly met a Jew means that as many as ten million residents of the country have had no contact with a Jew.

Table 5.1

Contact with Jews, 1983-1985

Contact	1983	1984	1985
often	16	17	16
occasionally	21	22	22
rarely	20	18	18
never	40	39	43
don't know	3	4	1
total	100% (2011)	100% (2038)	100% (1054)

Source: The 1983 and 1984 data are taken from H. Taylor Buckner, "The League for Human Rights of B'nai Brith Project on Anti-Semitism: A Study of Canadian Attitudes Towards Jews, Italians, and Poles - A Preliminary Comparative Analysis" *The Review of Anti-Semitism* (Toronto: League for Human Rights, 1984).

Interpretation: The level of personal contact with Jews remained relatively constant over the three years.

Table 5.2

Contact with Ethnic Groups, 1985

Contact	Italians	Blacks	Asians	Germans	Scots	Jews
often	24	17	17	23	30	16
occasionally	25	30	23	25	24	22
rarely	15	18	16	14	11	18
never	35	35	43	37	34	43
don't know	0	1	1	1	1	1
total	100%	100%	100%	100%	100%	100%

Sample size = 1054

Interpretation: Canadians reported appreciably less contact with Jews and Asians than with other ethnic groups.

To measure basic prejudice agaisnt Jews and against the five other ethnic groups, we asked respondents the following question: *"Would you say that members of the following ethnic groups have too much power, just enough power, or not enough power in Canada?"* As we explained earlier, whether a group is perceived as having too much or just the right amount of power depends more on how the group is looked upon than on how much power it actually has. Indeed, there is a fundamental paradox that any ethnic group which is considered too powerful by a majority in a democratic country cannot possibly be powerful because its unpopularity limits its ability to persuade the majority to accepts its leadership. Real power, after all, requires consent.

Periodic national surveys in the United States showed that Jews were most apt to be seen as powerful in the wake of the Holocaust, which demonstrated their actual impotence, and were least apt to be seen as powerful in more recent years, when the Jewish presence in the universities and professions was no longer negligible. In recent years, Japanese Americans were less apt to be considered powerful than American blacks although Japanese Americans have been over-represented statistically in high earning and influential positions while blacks have been under-represented. When people say that a group is too powerful, they are saying that it does not deserve whatever power they believe that it actually has.

Canadians were asked to assess the power of Italians, Blacks, Asians, Germans, Scots, and Jews (see fig. 5.1 and table 5.3). Jews were more apt to be identified as "too powerful" than any other group. The proportion saying that Jews were too powerful was 15% as compared to 13% for Italians, 10% for Asians, 7% for Blacks, 7% for Germans, and 6% for Scots.

Social scientists have long held that contact between people – building bridges – helps to lower bariers to mistrust and hostility. Personal contact provides a human face to a category of people. The effect of contact is to enable people to see members of the outgroup as having the same complexity of life styles, motivations, and needs as members of one's own group. Contact is especially important in the case of those outgroups about whom considerable negative information has already been received. In the case of Jews, Canadians and citizens of other Western nations do have some information even if they have never met a Jew. Some of the information may be theologically derived, about the putative role of ancient Jews in killing Jesus or about the refusal of Jews, then and now, to follow his way. Some of the information may be hearsay about various unsavory characteristics which contemporary Jews are alleged to have.

To find out if indeed contact with Jews reduces prejudice, we compared the percent saying that Jews have "too much" power for each level of contact (see fig. 5.2 and table 5.4). For each of the years, for 1983, 1984, and

1985, Canadians who reported never having any contact with a Jew were somewhat more apt to say that Jews had too much power. In 1985, people who had never met a Jew were almost 50% more likely to say that Jews had too much power than those who had met a Jew.

The data suggests that prejudice tends to dissolve in the face of at least some contact with Jews. But, it is unclear whether more and more contact necessarily produces less and less prejudice. Respondents were asked if they interacted with Jews "never", "rarely", "occasionally", or "often." The hypothesis that contact lowers prejudice is supported by the evidence that respondents with occasional contact were less prejudiced than those with rare contact, who were in turn less prejudiced than those with no contact at all. However, respondents who said that they "often" had contact with Jews were slightly more apt to be prejudiced than those who reported only "occasional" contact.

Unfortunately, the terms "rarely", "occasionally", and "often" are imprecise terms. We cannot be sure whether rare contact amounts to once a year, occasional contact five times a year, and frequent contact (i.e. "often") twenty times a year. Prejudiced people tend to see others in terms of group stereotypes and tend to be conscious of the group identity of the people they encounter. Thus, the group consciousness of some prejudiced respondents may lead them to exaggerate the frequency with which they encounter members of the group towards which they are prejudiced. In the answers of some prejudiced respondents, the word "often" may reflect group attitudes as well as actual frequency of contact.

Fig 5.1

PERCEIVED POWER OF ETHNIC GROUPS

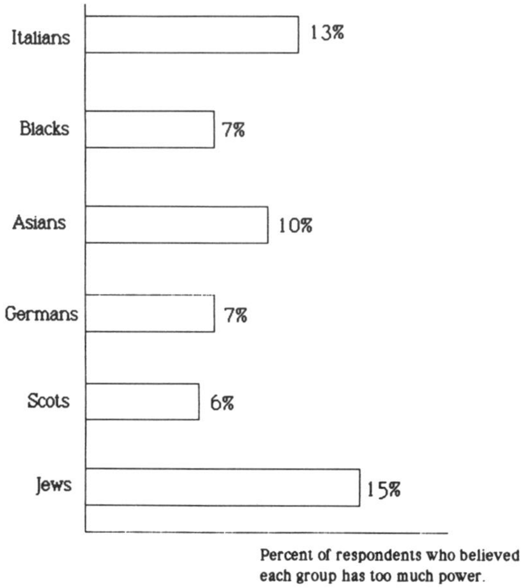

Interpretation: Jews and Italians are more often perceived to have "too much" power.

Fig 5.2

CONTACT WITH JEWS AND PERCEPTIONS OF POWER, 1985

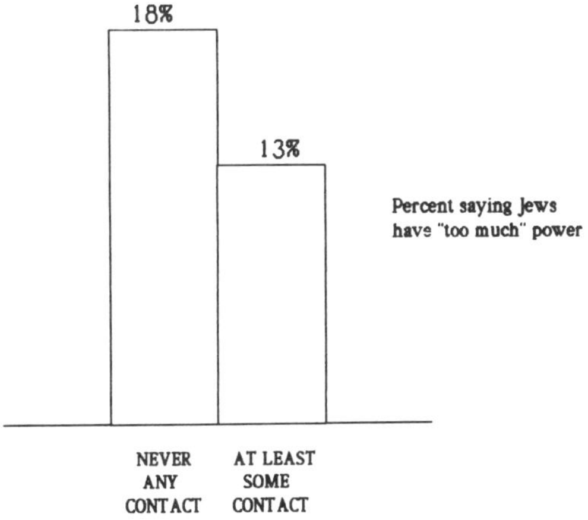

Interpretation: Canadians who have never met a Jew are more apt to think Jews have too much power.

Table 5.3

The Perceived Power of Ethnic Groups in Canada

Power	Italians	Blacks	Asians	Germans	Scots	Jews
too much	13	7	10	7	6	15
just enough	55	45	45	54	56	51
not enough	5	21	13	7	7	6
don't know	27	27	33	32	31	28
total	100% (1048)	100% (1049)	100% (1049)	100% (1049)	100% (1049)	100% (1049)

Table 5.4

Contact and the Image of the "Powerful" Jew

(Percent saying Jews have "too much" power)

Contact	1983	1984	1985
never	18	14	18
rarely	13	13	13
occasionally	11	11	11
often	14	14	14

Interpretation: In each year, those with some contact were less apt to be prejudiced.

The fact that personal contact reduces prejudice provides strong indirect evidence for the claim made in the previous chapter on the media, that media coverage of nonviolent Jewish events can affect how people feel about Jews. Those critics of television who are profoundly disenchanted with the medium have claimed that viewers in the media age know more about the health and wellbeing of talk host Johnny Carson than about their next door neighbours. Television can provide viewers with a certain kind of intimacy and can teach people about some complexities in the world outside the home. The previous chapter suggestion that English Canadians were more apt to become sympathetic to Jews than French Canadians in small part because the English media (except for Newfoundland) provided considerable coverage of nonviolent Jewish events while the French media provided none at all. English

Canadians have had two ways of learning about the humanity of Jewish life – personal contact and television.

Beyond the fact that contact with Jews does reduce the size of the prejudiced minority in the Canadian population, the national survey data point to two other facts. The size of the prejudiced minority is stable – it did not change very much from 1983 to 1985. Furthermore, although contact with Jews diminishes prejudice, it does not eliminate it altogether.

Social scientists have thought not only that contact between groups reduces prejudice but that people who are prejudiced against one group are prejudiced against all other outgroups at the same time. Archie Bunker of television fame was not merely anti-black. He was also anti-Jewish, anti-Asian, anti-foreign, anti-woman, and anti-student.

To discover whether prejudiced Canadians are generally hostile to all groups at once, we calculated coefficients of correlation among the attitudes to each of the six ethnic groups. Mathematically, a coefficient of correlation can range from −1.0 to +1.0. If people who are highly prejudiced against one ethnic group are also highly prejudiced against a second ethnic gorup, we should find a plus correlation between the two attitudes which is as close to +1.0 as possible. If people who are highly prejudiced against one group are not at all prejudiced against a second group, we should find a minus correlation between the two attitudes which is as close as possible to −1.0. If only some of the people prejudiced against the first group are also prejudiced against the second, we should find a plus or minus correlation which is as close to 0 as possible. In our analysis, ethnocentrism or hostility to each group was measured by whether the respondent thought the group had too much power.

Table 5.5 contains the coefficients of correlation for contact with each of the six ethnic groups and the coefficient of correlations for prejudice against each of the six groups. The correlation coefficients for contact with members of each of the six groups vary very little. They all hover around +.53. The fact that the correlation coefficients for inter-group contact are all approximately +.5 shows that people who have contact with one particular group tend to have contact with members of every other group. The fact that the coefficients cluster together and do not differ greatly suggests that contact with ethnic groups has no pattern. People who meet Asians are no more likely to meet Jews and Italians, lets say, than Germans and Scots.

The correlation coefficients for prejudice against the six groups show a slightly different pattern. The correlations for prejudice are all in the +.5 to +.8 range. All the coefficients have plus rather than minus signs. This means that people hostile to one group tend to be hostile to them all. However, prejudice against Jews is only moderately correlated with prejudice against the other five groups. For example, the correlation between anti-Italian and anti-Jewish prejudice is a moderate +.54 while the correlation between anti-Italian and anti-Black prejudice is a high +.71. The correlation between anti-German and anti-Jewish prejudice is +.51 while the correlation between anti-German and anti-Scottish prejudice is a high of +.82. Thus, prejudice against Jews is not quite like prejudice against the other groups. Prejudice against Jews has an element in common with the other five prejudices, but it also has to some extent a life of its own.[4]

Table 5.5

Correlation Coefficients for Contact With and Prejudice Against Six Ethnic Groups, 1985

Contact

	Jews	Italians	Blacks	Asians	Germans	Scots
Jews	-	.59	.56	.56	.50	.51
Italians	-	-	.59	.51	.48	.50
Blacks	-	-	-	.58	.47	.47
Asians	-	-	-	-	.52	.48
Germans	-	-	-	-	-	.60
Scots	-	-	-	-	-	-

Prejudice (i.e. perceived power)

	Jews	Italians	Blacks	Asians	Germans	Scots
Jews	-	.54	.51	.49	.51	.51
Italians	-	-	.71	.67	.67	.65
Blacks	-	-	-	.71	.72	.71
Asians	-	-	-	-	.73	.71
Germans	-	-	-	-	-	.82
Scots	-	-	-	-	-	-

Interpretation: (1) People in contact with one ethnic group are apt to be in contact with all. (2) People prejudiced against any one group are apt to be prejudiced against the others except that prejudice against Jews has to some extent a life of its own. (3) Statistically minded readers may note that all correlations are significant at the .001 level.

Much of what social scientists know about ethnic attitudes was developed in the wake of the Holocaust, as an attempt to explain how an otherwise civilized nation, Germany, could do so much evil. American sociologists and psychologists produced two concepts – the theory of the authoritarian personality and the theory of ethnocentrism.[5] The theory of the authoritarian personality provided evidence of a personality type, a rigid person who harboured intense hostility and aggression which he could barely disguise from strangers. The authoritarian person displayed abject obedience to superiors and ruthless domination over subordinates. Authoritarian people tended to be ethnocentric. They were hostile towards and prejudiced against members of all groups other than their own.

Social scient ists have shown time and again that ethnocentric people hate all outgroups and hate them with roughly equal intensity. Our data conform to the accepted understanding of ethnocentrism but with slight differences. Our data show that the very essence of ethnocentrism is hate, not discomfort with ethnic groups which appear to be different in a cultural, racial, or religious way. Our survey asked for people's feelings about five bottom dog groups and one topdog group, the Scots.

Anglo-Scots have long occupied a privileged place in Canadian history and continue to occupy a central place in the corporate and government establishments.[6] If ethnocentrism were hostility against outgroups only, we would expect no correlation between hostility to Scots on the one hand and hostility to Asians, Blacks, Italians, and Jews on the other hand. We would not really expect any prejudice against Scots. If any prejudice were expressed against Scots, we would not expect it to come from the same people who are prejudiced against the other groups.

However, the survey tells a different story. The survey shows that Canadians are not free of prejudice against Scots (fig. 5.1) and that prejudice against Scots comes from the same quarters as prejudice against the other groups. The following chapter will show that even Presbyterians are hostile against Scots although members of this Protestant denomination are themselves largely of Scottish origin. The lesson from all this is that ethnocentrism reflects an undercurrent of hate and aggression. Ethnocentric people are haters who may hate their own group too but feel legitimate and relatively safe from reprisal when acting out their hate against weak outsiders.

Most studies of ethnocentrism have placed an empahsis on the indiscriminant nature of ethnic hostility. For example, people who hate Blacks also hate Asians. Our survey suggests a slight amendment. The data show that hatred against Jews has to some extent a life of its own. Given that Jews are distinguished from other groups not by language or skin colour but by religion, some of the roots of anti-Judaism even today may be religious.

Our next step in this chapter is to explore how domestic anti-Judaism ("too much" power in Canada) is related to beliefs about the Holocaust. We employed several different statistical procedures to assess whether the same people tend to choose anti-Jewish answers on the various Jewish questions. For example, we used a complex procedure known as factor analysis to reveal the structure of anti-Jewish prejudice. The data did show a single underlying pattern of thinking. People who were prejudiced on the domestic question of power were also prejudiced on the Holocaust issues and vice-versa.

We are not reporting the results of our complex factor analysis but will describe in a simpler way how domestic anti-Judaism and Holocaust anti-Judaism are related. Fig. 5.3 and table 5.6 show that people who believe that Jews have too much power in Canadian society are more likely than other Canadians to say that the Holocaust was at least partly the Jews' fault or to say that they do not know how to apportion blame. Fig. 5.3 shows that the proportion who blame the Holocaust on Jews is 31% among those who see Jews as having too much power and only 16% among those who say that Jews have "just enough" power. Fig. 5.3 also shows that the proportion who say that the six million estimate is too high is 28% among people who say that Jews have too much power and only 13% among those who say that Jews have just enough power. Altogether, people who are prejudiced against Jews in a Canadian context are twice as likely to voice a Holocaust "revisionist" perspective as those who are not prejudiced in a domestic context.

Fig 5.3

HOLOCAUST ANTI-JUDAISM AND DOMESTIC ANTI-JUDAISM: THEIR RELATIONSHIP

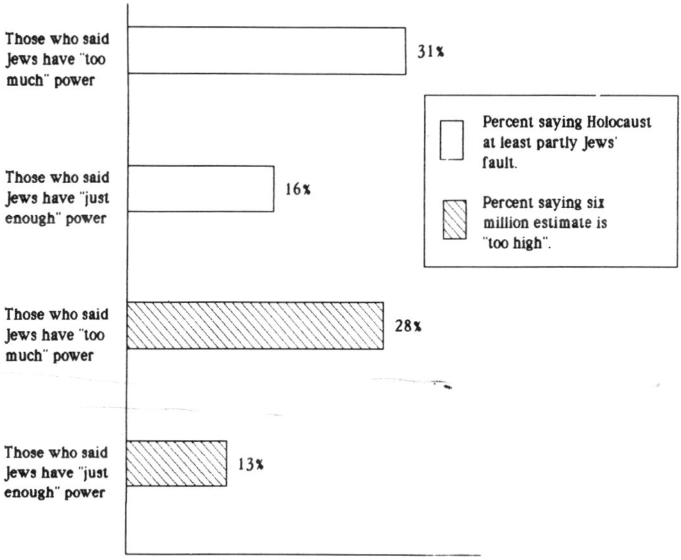

Interpretation: People prejudiced against Jews in a Canadian context were apt to be prejudiced in a Holocaust context, and vice-versa.

Table 5.6

The Co-Relationship among Anti-Jewish Prejudices

(row percents)

Power of Jews	Holocaust is Jews' fault	Holocaust is Not J. fault	Six Million estimate Too high	Six Million estimate About right
"too much"	31%	45%	28%	44%
"just enough"	16%	68%	13%	59%

Interpretation: People who were prejudiced on one question were apt to be on the others as well. People who thought that Jews have too much power in Canada today were twice as likely to blame Jews for the Holocaust or say that the six million estimate was excessive.

Anti-Jewish sentiment is not random or haphazard. It has a structure. People who felt that Jews are too powerful in Canada were more likely to blame the Holocaust on its victims and to say that the six million estimate was too high. We did not specifically ask respondents if they thought that Jews in Europe were too powerful. But, it is probably a reasonable supposition that respondents who thought that Canadian Jews were too powerful also thought that European Jews were too powerful. The existence of a pattern of anti-Jewish prejudice shows that prejudiced respondents tended to be logical and consistent even if they tended to be poorly educated and ill-informed.

The strongly related pattern of response to the three Jewish questions (power, blame, and estimated casualties) permitted us to construct an anti-Jewish index or scale in order to reflect the intensity of anti-Jewish feeling. The anti-Jewish index or scale was built by adding the respondents' answers to the three questions. A score of zero was assigned to a nonhostile respondent, who refused to say that Jews had too much power or were to blame for the Holocaust or that fewer than six million died. A score of "1" was assigned to a respondent who opted for one out of the three possible anti-Jewish answers. The highest possible score of "3" was given to someone who chose all three hostile answers.

Fig. 5.4 displays the number of Canadians who voiced varying degrees of anti-Jewish feeling. The largest group was the 63% who were completely devoid of hostility. One-quarter of the sample chose one of three possible hostile responses while 1% was unflinchingly hostile. Altogether, a large minority – 37% – were prepared to offer at least one prejudiced response.

Fig 5.4

THE DISTRIBUTION OF CANADIANS ON THE PREJUDICE INDEX.

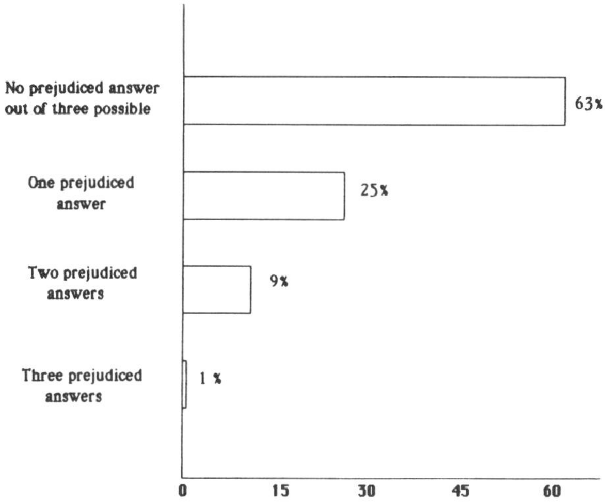

Interpretation: Only 63% of Canadians are entirely free of anti-Jewish prejudice.

Fig 5.5

THE DISTRIBUTION OF CANADIANS
ON THE IGNORANCE INDEX.

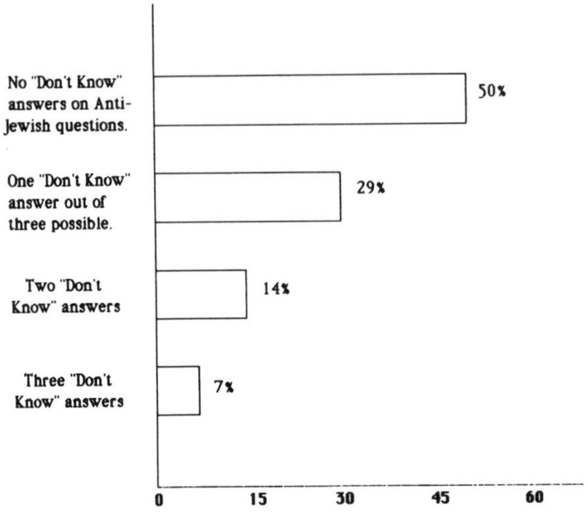

Interpretation: Only half of Canadians avoided "don't know" answers on questions measuring anti-Jewish prejudice.

The Eichmann study in the United States also constructed an index or scale of anti-Jewish prejudice based on the responses to three questions measuring prejudice. Because the American index used slightly different questions, a detailed comparison between the Canadian and American results would not make much sense.[7] However, it is noteworthy that the patterns in the two countries were not very different. In Canada, 63% avoided prejudiced answers as compared to 56% in the United States a generation earlier. In both countries, the size of the slightly prejudiced community – those who chose one hostile answer out of three – was the same, one fourth.

To this point, our analysis has focussed on prejudice as an open and frank expression of antagonism. When a person says that Jews were to blame for the Holocaust, there is little room left for interpretation. However, suppose a person says that he or she does not know whether Jews were to blame for the Holocaust. Saying that one does not know may be a candid admission of a lack of knowledge or it may be a disguised form of hostility or a combination of the two. Even if those who say that they "don't know" are being entirely candid, this is an undesirable situation. Innocent ignorance is fertile ground for the cultivation of prejudice.

Following the model of the index of anti-Jewish prejudice, we created an index of acknowledged ignorance. The ignorance index was based on "don't know" responses to the questions used in the anti-Jewish index. A respondent was assigned a score of "0" if he or she never acknowledged not knowing. Respondents who replied "don't know" to the three questions about Jewish power, blame for the Holocaust, and the six million estimate received the maximum score of "3". Fig. 5.5 shows that half of Canadians admit to not knowing how to answer at least one of these three questions. That as many as half of Canadians acknowledge not knowing is a remarkable statistic.

Our next step was to apply the two indices – prejudice and admitted ignorance – in a joint fashion. The joint application of the two indices produced four groups of Canadians:

1. those who are *prejudiced;* members of this group chose at least one anti-Jewish answer but do not admit not knowing an answer.
2. those who are *ignorant*; members of this group admitted not knowing at least once (i.e. at least one "don't know" answer), but never chose an anti-Jewish answer.
3. Those who are *prejudiced* and are *ignorant*; members of this group chose at least one hostile answer and at least one "don't know" answer.
4. The *civic* group; members of this group avoided all hostile and "don't know" answers.

The largest group were those who frankly admitted their lack of knowledge or ignorance without adopting any hostile responses (group #2). This group of wellmeaning but uninformed people represent a sizeable 38% of the country. This is the group which should be the target of educational efforts by television, the schools, and Jewish community organizations. This strictly uninformed group outnumbered the group of informed, nonhostile citizens, who placed second with 35% of the population (group #4). The third position was occupied by the prejudiced group (group #1). The prejudiced group consists of the 16% who chose at least one prejudiced answer but no "don't knows." In fourth and last position were the 11% who revealed both hate and ignorance (group #3). They chose at least one hostile answer as well as at least one "don't know" answer.

Analysing the pattern of prejudice in conjunction with the pattern of avowed ignorance leads to the conclusion that anti-Judaism is a serious problem in this country. Altogether, 27% of the Canadian population either displays prejudice against Jews or displays both prejudice and admitted ignorance. An additional 38% of the population constitutes fertile ground for prejudice because of an admitted lack of information on such elementary issues as whether Jews were responsible for the Holocaust. Only 35% of the population constitutes an informed, unprejudiced citizenry.

Table 5.7

Provincial Frequencies (in percent) on the Indices of Prejudice and Admitted Ignorance

(a) Anti-Judaism Index

Scores	Nfld.	N.S.	N.B.	Que.	Ont.	Man.	Sask.	Alta.	B.C.
0	74	80	58	64	71	73	90	81	89
1	16	17	35	30	24	25	8	14	9
2-3	10	3	8	7	4	3	2	5	2
total	100%	100%	100%	100%	100%	100%	100%	100%	100%
	(31)	(30)	(40)	(253)	(364)	(40)	(50)	(99)	(122)

(b) Admitted Ignorance Index

Scores	Nfld.	N.S.	N.B.	Que.	Ont.	Man.	Sask.	Alta.	B.C.
0	32	53	40	52	52	48	54	55	44
1	13	23	23	30	29	25	32	21	38
2-3	55	23	38	18	18	28	14	24	15
total	100%	100%	100%	100%	100%	100%	100%	100%	100%
	(31)	(30)	(40)	(263)	(364)	(40)	(50)	(99)	(122)

Interpretation: Newfoundland and New Brunswick show high rates of both prejudice and acknowledged ignorance while Quebec shows only a high rate of prejudice.

Figs. 5.6 and 5.7 and table 5.7 display the pattern of prejudice and admitted lack of information among the provinces. Provincial comparisons are important because, under the Canadian constitution, provincial governments possess exclusive responsibility for schooling. Through their control of education, provincial governments have enormous opportunities to convey information to young people which can increase their level of knowledge and reduce their level of prejudice.

Our survey data shows that very large majorities are devoid of any anti-Jewish prejudice in Saskatchewan (90%), British Columbia (89%), Alberta (81%), and Nova Scotia (80%). By contrast, the provinces with the smallest majorities free of anti-Jewish prejudice are New Brunswick (58%) and Quebec (64%). These two provinces have very large minorities with a moderate degree of prejudice and significant minorities with intense prejudices. Alberta represents a curious picture of polarization betwen a very large, informed, unprejudiced majority and a moderately large minority of intensely prejudiced people. Like Alberta, neighbouring British Columbia

Fig 5.6

THE FREQUENCY OF EXTREME PREJUDICE AMONG THE PROVINCES

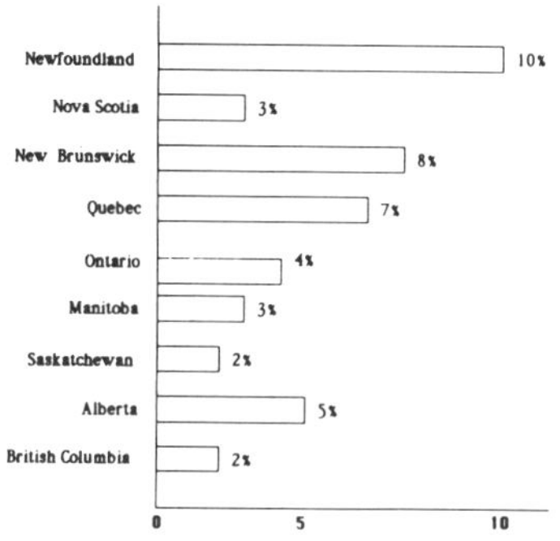

Interpretation: Extreme anti-Jewish prejudice occurs more frequently in Newfoundland, New Brunswick, Quebec and to some extent in Alberta.

Fig 5.7

THE FREQUENCY OF ADMITTED IGNORANCE AMONG THE PROVINCES

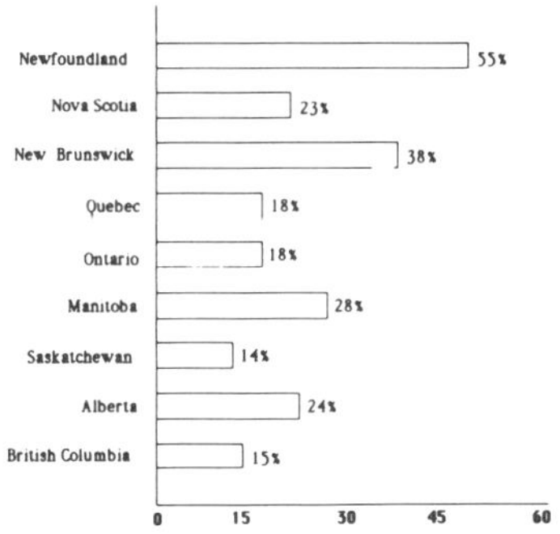

Interpretation: When fig 5.7 and fig 5.6 are compared, it is noteworthy that prejudice and admitted ignorance occur more frequently in Newfoundland and New Brunswick. In Quebec, prejudice occurs without an accompanying acknowledgement of ignorance.

and Saskatchewan have large majorities of nonhostile citizens. But, B.C. and Saskatchewan have 2% or fewer of highly prejudiced people while the proportion in Alberta is 5%.

In order to have a simple measure of prejudice in the nine provinces, we calculated a prejudice score, taking into consideration the number of people in each province who were not at all prejudiced, somewhat prejudiced, or very prejudiced. With the score for each province provided in parenthesis, we can rank order the provinces from least to most prejudiced as follows:

Almost unprejudiced	(British Columbia (score of 0.11) (Saskatchewan (0.12)
Moderately prejudiced	(Nova Scotia (0.22) (Alberta (0.24) (Manitoba (0.30) (Ontario (0.32) (Newfoundland (0.35)
Highly prejudiced	(Quebec (0.43) (New Brunswick (0.50)

The pattern of prejudice scores suggests that New Brunswick and Quebec require the most immediate educational attention, followed by Newfoundland, Ontario and perhaps Manitoba. Although Keegstra and Eckville put Alberta in the headlines for months and years, Alberta is not a pressing problem by national standards.

It is one thing to identify provincial concentrations of prejudice. It is quite another to persuade prejudiced people to think in more rational and democratic ways. People who openly admit their ignorance may be more reachable than those who are more confident about their knowledge. Following the pattern of hate scores for each province, we also calculated ignorance scores. With their ignorance scores in parenthesis, the nine provinces are ranked from low ignorance to high ignorance as follows:

low admitted ignorance	(Saskatchewan (.60) (Ontario (0.65) (Quebec (0.66) (Nova Scotia (0.66) (British Columbia (0.67) (Alberta (0.69)
high admitted ignorance	(Manitoba (0.80) (New Brunswick (0.96) (Newfoundland (1.21)

The provincial scores of prejudice and admitted lack of knowledge can be married together in order to produce a guide to where the most effective educational efforts could be undertaken. Fig. 5.8 shows how the provinces can be classified by means of both prejudice and ignorance. The cell for the most prejudiced and most ignorant province is occupied by New Brunswick. New Brunswick ought to be the first target of educational efforts and educational reform designed to improve inter-group relations. The residents of New Brunswick are important to reach because of their high degree of prejudice. They may be reachable because of their ready willingness to admit ignorance. Quebec is important because of its high degree of prejudice and because of its large population and political influence within the country. However, Quebecers may be less reachable than Newfoundlanders and Manitobans, who express less hostility and acknowledge more readily their ignorance. Ontario should also be the subject of educational efforts. Although Ontario is found among the category of moderately prejudiced provinces, its score is relatively high for this category.

Table 5.8

Classifying Provinces According to Both Anti-Judaism and Ignorance

		Admitted Ignorance Index: Low	Admitted Ignorance Index: High
Anti-Judaism Index	Low	Saskatchewan British Columbia	
	Medium	Nova Scotia Alberta Ontario	Manitoba Newfoundland
	High	Quebec	New Brunswick

To identify those provinces which show high rates of anti-Jewish prejudice or high rates of admitted ignorance has a practical usefulness. Knowing which provinces have the more serious problems can help governments, educational authorities, civil liberty groups, the Canadian Council of Christians and Jews, and Jewish communal groups know where to put their resources. However, knowing that a province is more hostile than another does not explain the origin of that hostility. If Quebec and New Brunswick are more hostile than Saskatchewan and British Columbia, the answer does not lie in the presence of the St. Lawrence river or in the soil of East-central Canada. Any real explanation for the different levels of prejudice among the Canadian provinces must lie in the kinds of people who inhabit the provinces and how they see the world. The ensuing chapter looks in greater detail at the nature of anti-Judaism in Canada, at the kinds of people who are prejudiced and why.

1 We term the reinforcement of existing attitudes towards Jews among francophones a *nonpositive* effect because it is to some extent an ambiguous philosophical question whether the reinforcement of an attitude which is partly neutral and partly negative should be described as strictly neutral or negative-neutral.

2 H. Taylor Buckner, "The League for Human Rights of B'nai Brith Canada Research Project on Anti-Semitism: A Study of Canadian Attitudes Towards Jews, Italians and Poles - A Preliminary Comparative Analysis, 1983 and 1984" in *The Review of Anti-Semitism in Canada* (Toronto: League for Human Rights, 1984).

3 See Frances Henry and Effie Ginsberg, "Who Gets the Work: A Test of Racial Discrimination in Employment" (Toronto: Urban Alliance on Race Relations and the Social Planning Council of Metropolitan Toronto, 1985).

4 Statistically minded readers may note that the correlations were tested for significant difference among them. The only significant differences were between the coefficients on the first line of table 5.5 (Jews) and the others (significant at the .001 level). Differences among the other coefficients were not significant at the .05 level.

5 For a critical overview of the classic work on *The Authoritarian Personality* by T. Adorno *et al.*, see Richard Christie and Marie Jahoda, *Studies in the Scope and Method of 'The Authoritarian Personality'* (Glencoe, Ill.: Free Press, 1954). See also Tomas Blass, ed., *Personality Variables in Social Behavior* (Toronto: Wiley, 1977).

6 For the classic statement on this matter, see John Porter, *The Vertical Mosaic: An Analysis of Social Class and Power in Canada* (Toronto: University of Toronto Press, 1968).

7 Glock *et al.*, *The Apathetic Majority,* pp. 41-2/

Chapter 6

Profile of Anti-Jewish Prejudice in Canada

Overview

The first step in discovering why people hold the attitudes which they do is to identify the kinds of people who are most apt to hold these attitudes. The early part of this chapter identifies the kinds of Canadians who are most apt to harbour anti-Jewish sentiments. We examine mainly the role of age, education, gender, religion, and language. The later part of the chapter compares the kinds of people who are anti-Jewish while being generally ethnocentric and the kinds of people who tend to be singlemindedly anti-Jewish.

Age

Age can play a role in the acquisition of attitudes in at least two different ways. Different age groups or cohorts can hold different views because of the period in which they grew up. People whose late adolescent or early adult years were in the Great Depression, it is often said, were anxious to protect their own children from any material privations which resembled their own. Age can also affect what people believe in the sense that the bodies and minds of people change as they grow older. For example, young people, particularly young males, are almost always more susceptible to the attractions of revolutionary movements than their elders. Young males were the backbone of Germany's Nazi movement as they were also of various Communist revolutions around the world.[1]

The national opinion data show that people in their middle years, those aged 40 to 50, are apt to be somewhat less prejudiced against Jews than those older and than those younger than themselves. For example, approximately 13% of those aged 40-59 said that Jews have too much power as compared to 18% among those 60+ and 16% among those younger than 40. Those older than 59 or younger than 25 were more apt to think that the six million estimate was exaggerated. The question which really highlighted age differences was the item about responsibility for the Holocaust. In the 40-49 age group, very few said that they did not know who was responsible and only 11% blamed Jews in any way. The number blaming Jews grew to almost twice as large in the 25-39 age group (19%) and was exactly twice as large in the under 25 age group (22%). Respondents in the 60+ age group were also more likely to blame Jews (15%) (see fig. 6.1 and table 6.1).

Fig 6.1

BLAMING JEWS FOR THE HOLOCAUST AMONG AGE GROUPS.

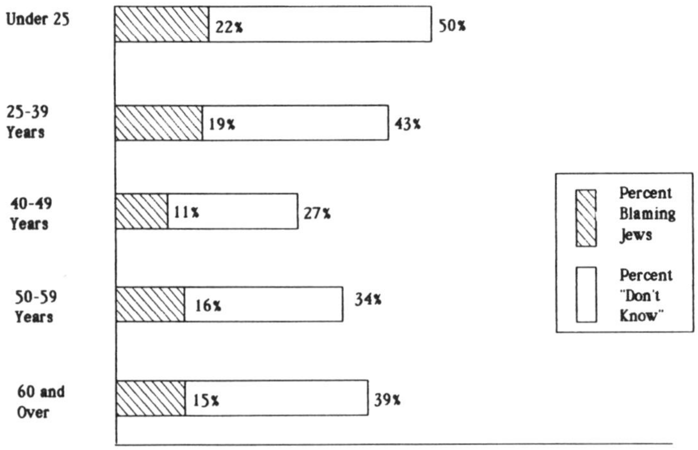

Interpretation: The young and the old are more prejudiced with respect to the Holocaust.

Table 6.1 Anti-Jewish Prejudice among Different Demographic Groups

	Jewish Power		6 Million Est.		Holocaust J. Fault	
	% "too much"	% don't know	% too much	% don't know	% mostly/partly Jews' fault	% don't know
Age						
under 25	15	30	19	33	22	28
25-39	17	30	15	30	19	23
40-49	14	27	15	20	11	16
50-59	12	27	12	28	16	18
60+	18	23	17	25	15	24
Sex						
male	18	20	15	28	20	19
female	13	35	16	27	14	25
Education						
pub. sch.	2	32	19	40	5	38
sec. sch.	16	30	7	27	18	25
post-sec.	13	22	13	20	17	10
university	0	22	11	24	17	11
Income						
under $10M*	12	38	22	37	19	27
$10M-14.99	20	28	21	24	17	20
$15M-19.99	17	31	15	23	18	23
$20M-29.99	13	22	13	30	17	23
$30M-39.99	15	21	10	26	20	15
over $40M	17	19	14	21	17	15
Occupation						
professional	14	19	14	22	22	13
business ex.	18	17	10	23	15	13
sales	18	20	9	22	20	18
clerical	13	34	12	27	14	19
skilled labour	18	21	14	34	18	26
unskil. labour	21	26	19	35	12	24
unemployed	11	35	8	30	11	32
housewife	12	38	18	27	16	29
student	12	25	19	15	12	9
Language						
English	12	25	12	26	18	16
French	21	22	23	29	15	31
Province						
Nfld.	16	39	16	48	10	55
N.S.	13	37	10	23	20	20
N.B.	25	25	25	38	18	48
Quebec	19	19	21	24	16	27
Ontario	17	28	15	28	18	16
Manitoba	20	35	10	33	25	30
Sask.	4	26	6	24	12	14
Alberta	12	28	12	28	17	21
B.C.	3	38	8	26	15	15

Religion						
Anglican	9	33	11	33	15	23
United	16	24	9	27	22	14
Baptist	13	30	13	35	13	17
Lutheran	3	28	14	14	14	14
Presbyt.	17	29	17	38	25	33
Other Prot.	8	37	11	28	13	23
Catholic	22	23	21	26	18	26
Eng. Cath.	18	21	17	23	13	12
Fr. Cath.	23	28	24	28	32	33

* The first two categories are under $10,000 and between $10,000 and $14,999.

Interpretation: see the text.

The greater prejudices of the older generation are relatively easy to explain in terms of the climate of political and social opinion during their formative years. The bulk of the oldest cohort group in our study would have experienced their late teen and early adult life during the "dirty thirties". Following on the heels of the Depression, the 1930's were marked by a climate of fear and intolerance which included a paranoid anti-Communism, xenophobia, and anti-Judaism. Fascist clubs were encouraged, organized, and funded across the country by Mussolini's Italy and by the new Nazi state.[2] Within Quebec, the Catholic church was anxious about the secular threats of big city life and tended to see Judaism as part of the problem. In 1932, the displeasure of the Bishops obliged the Quebec Liberal government to abolish legislation setting up Jewish Committees to advise the Protestant and Catholic school boards on how to educate Jewish children. There were no Jewish school boards.[3] The Church also wanted all Jews, Canadian- or foreign-born, to have their citizenship taken away.[4]

In English Canada, anti-Jewish ideas became fashionable, especially among those who modelled themselves on the Tory upper class of Britain. For upper crust Englishmen and English Canadians in the 30's, anti-Judaism was desirable both in itself and as a means of thwarting what was sometimes perceived as a joint liberal-welfarist-bolshevik menace. Signs were erected at Montreal and Toronto beaches, proclaiming "No Jews and Dogs Allowed". Charlotte Whitton, then a prominent social worker and later to be mayor of the nation's capital, traversed the country warning of the dangers of admitting Jewish orphans as refugees from Nazism. Prime Minister Mackenzie King confided to his diary that he could not help but think that the election of Hitler was a good thing for Germany. The climate of prejudice was such that the ministers and mandarins of the federal government endeavored to prevent Jewish refugees from finding safety in this country before the Holocaust and connived even to prevent the survivors from immigrating after the war.[5]

Canadians who are today between 40 and 59 years of age grew up in the late 1940's and in the 1950's. The newsreels in the post-war cinemas made clear who were the destroyers and who were the destroyed. The rebirth of Israel in 1948 earned Canadian Jews respect because the erstwhile victims could strike back. That same year, Canadians of Asian descent were granted the full franchise. Ten years earlier, in 1938, Asian Canadians had had their limited rights eroded further.[6] In 1950, Canada embarked on a decade of growth in material welfare and cultural tolerance. In 1957, voters chose as Prime Minister John Diefenbaker, a man who identified with ethnic Canada. Diefenbaker embraced the Black cause in South Africa, the Jewish cause in Israel, and the Ukrainian cause in USSR. During the 1960's, 1970's and 1980's, Canada welcomed large influxes of non-white immigrants from the Pacific rim, the Caribbean, and South Asia. Canada became increasingly a "multicultural" society in demographic reality and was recognised as such in government pronouncements. Given the very different political and social climates of the pre- and post-war years, it is not surprising that Canadians who today are in their forties should be much less prejudiced than those who are now at least 60 years old.

It is a more difficult task to explain why the youngest generations are more prejudiced. This task is also more important. It is alarming that *as many as half of Canadians under 25 years old do not explicitly hold Jews blameless for their victimization*. The 50% of under 25 year olds who avoid saying that Jews were innocent is almost double the rate among people presently in their forties (27%). The youngest generation, those under 25, are also the most likely to deny or be uncertain that six million died. However, the youngest are not especially more apt to say that Jews have too much power in Canada today. Thus, the prejudice of the young focuses on the Holocaust as an event in history rather than on the role of Canadian Jews today.

There are countless possible explanations for the attitudes of the young. One explanation is that young people are much farther removed historically from the events of the Nazi period and thus less motivated to learn about it. For them, the Holocaust is "history", an item of strictly impersonal academic interest. Another possible explanation for prejudice among the young is that they may be a less moralistic generation. If true, the lesser moralism of the young may be explained by many different factors. It may be explained by their intensive exposure to television programming, by the range of pornography freely available to them, or by the moral relativism taught in the schools.

The moral relativism in the curriculum of the schools has been accompanied by a kind of factual relativism. In the age of the social sciences, people are no longer sure if even simple facts are facts. Are human beings motivated by conscious plans and purposes or are they motivated by deep unconscious urges of which they are only dimly aware? Does sending criminals to prison reform them, punish them, or harden them? Almost by their very nature, the social sciences teach factual uncertainty.

It may be unnecessary to point to moral or factual relativism as explanations for the Holocaust-related prejudice of the young. The simplest explanation may be that the young are unfamiliar with twentieth century European history and with the prolonged period of oppression of Jews dating from the crusades. Secondary schools usually skip over this extraordinary period in Western history or provide an ambiguous or ambivalent interpretation. People in their forties may have been able to learn in adulthood about the Holocaust and Europe's history of victimization from books and from public affairs and documentary programs on television.

Young people may begin their understanding of the Holocaust with the handicap of having learned about Jews in school from works which highlight Jewish rigidity or villainy. In Ontario, most high school students are introduced to Shakespeare by studying *The Merchant of Venice*. In addition, intermediate and senior students often study, as a formal part of their English curriculum, Charles Dickens' *Oliver Twist*. Both works focus on the careers of particularly repellant and abhorrent figures whose villainy is related directly to their Jewishness.

Writing at a time when Jews were still legally excluded from England, Shakespeare portrayed the archetypal Jew as found in medieval thought. In those countries where their presence was allowed, Jews were for centuries prohibited from undertaking farming and other profitable and respectable occupations as their punishment for deicide and for their "stiffnecked" refusal to replace the old faith with the new. Jews were legally the property of the rulers under whose jurisdiction they lived. They were restricted to certain banking and other trades which were then either unprofitable, dangerous, or unsuitable for Christian believers. Shakespeare's merchant Shylock was the theologically required Jew – unbending in his Jewish belief, failed in his efforts to keep his daughter from Christianity, wanting his "pound of flesh" in revenge, and preoccupied with his ducats (money).

Charles Dickens' Fagen is less interesting as a character but more interesting on account of the author. A Jew, Fagen is the book's central evil character, a master thief and manipulator of young boys. After *Oliver Twist* appeared in print, a Jewish lady explained to Dickens the broader meaning and consequences of his work. Contrite, Dickens then put pen to paper and wrote *Our Mutual Friend*, which contained a totally unblemished Jewish hero, who is made to appear villainous by the machinations of his Christian employer. Although *Our Mutual Friend* is generally acknowledged as a superior work by the standards of literary criticism, it is rarely if ever studied as part of a formal curriculum.[7] "Fagen" has entered the English language as a word denoting the adult head of an adolescent crime ring. "Shylock" has come to mean money-lender, especially, interestingly enough, in French Canada.

Without further research, it is not possible to be certain precisely why young people today are more likely than their elders to be unaware of the magnitude of the Holocaust or to be unable to draw the appropriate moral lessons. In the absence of further research, it makes most sense to do something about obvious factors in youthful ignorance. Educators and parents seeking to introduce Holocaust curricula should be given encouragement. So should educators and parents seeking to transfer the *Merchant of Venice* and *Oliver Twist* to upper years, where students are older and less impressionable, or to replace these works with less pejorative ones.

Gender

A recurrent theme in our examination of the response to the Zundel trial and in our present look at rates of anti-Jewish prejudice is that women are less hostile than men.[8] Men and women expressed approximately the same views on the magnitude of the casualties during the Holocaust. But, women were less apt to blame Jews (14% vs. 20%) and less apt to affirm that Jews have "too much" power in Canada today (13% vs. 18%).

The lower level of prejudice among women is especially noteworthy in view of the fact that women interact with Jews less often than men and that women have less education than men. If gender did not matter, the lower exposure to Jews and the lower education among women ought to have produced greater, not lesser, prejudice among women. As many as 49% of women reported never having met a Jew as compared to only 39% among men. Women were also less likely to have met members of other ethnic groups. For example, 41% of women claimed to have had no contact with Blacks as compared to 34% of men.

The lesser prejudice of women is more marked in the case of domestic prejudice (power in Canada) than in the case of the Holocaust and is especially evident when men and women are compared at the same levels of formal education. Fig. 6.2 shows that women with primary and secondary school education are less likely to be prejudiced and that prejudice is especially absent in the case of university educated women. *Male university graduates are more than three times more likely to believe that Jews are too powerful than female graduates (13% vs. 4%).* The rate of 4% among women graduates is a remarkable figure. If all Canadians were as unprejudiced as female graduates of universities, Canada would not have a problem of anti-Judaism.

Fig 6.2

THE PERCEIVED POWER OF JEWS
THROUGH MALE AND FEMALE EYES.
(% Saying "too much" power)

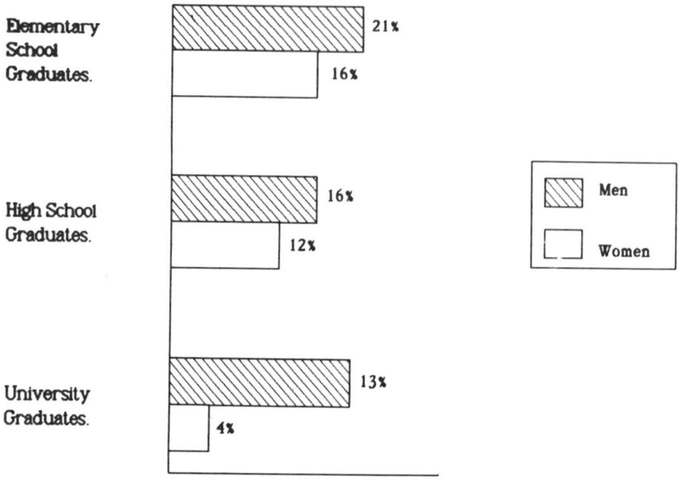

Interpretation: At every level of education, women are less prejudiced then men.

Although women in our sample were conspicuously less anti-Jewish than men, they were not conspicuously less prejudiced against the other five ethnic groups.[9] We are at a loss to explain why women were noticeably more friendly to Jews than other groups except for the possibility that these feelings may have been engendered by thought of the Holocaust or a perception of Jews as nonviolent or family-centered. The relative absence of anti-Jewish prejudice among women may also be explained by favourable images resulting from the strong presence of Jews in medicine, psychology, social work and other helping professions. Our respondents were asked about the power of the different groups at the very beginning of the interviews so that respondents could not have been motivated to speak favourably of Jewish power by thoughts of the Holocaust generated by the questionnaire itself.

Education

Throughout this study, we have noted a constructive role associated with education. People with greater education were especially apt to become aware of the trial and to become more sympathetic to Jews. Irrespective of the trial, people with more education were apt to be less prejudiced than people with less education. Public school leavers were more than twice as likely as university graduates to believe that Jews have "too much" power in Canada (21% vs. 10%). Public school leavers were almost twice as likely to declare that the six million estimate was exaggerated (19% vs. 11%). The number of public school leavers who did not know whom to blame for the Holocaust or who blamed Jews was also twice as high as among university graduates (53% vs. 27%).

In the case of responsibility for the Holocaust, a special caveat is in order. In the particular case of assigning blame for the tragedy, the principal difference between highly and poorly educated people is that very few of the highly educated admitted not knowing (11% vs. 38%). Among university graduates, people who otherwise might have said that they did not know whom to blame said instead that Jews were faultless. However, greater education did *not* reduce the size of the minority who held Jews at least partly responsible for their own victimization. The number of public school leavers who blamed the Jews was 15% as compared to 18% among high school graduates, 17% among those with some college, and 17% among university graduates. Against the fact that only 10% of university graduates saw Jews as having too much power, the fact that as many as 17% blamed the Jews for the Holocaust suggest that at least some of those who blamed Jews were not purposefully hostile. If one knows little about European history and the Holocaust, if one is a moral relativist believing that people are rarely completely right or completely wrong, and if one is a factual relativist doubting that facts are necessarily facts, it makes sense to assume that Jews must somehow share responsibility for whatever calamity may have befallen them.

To summarize, education does reduce prejudice but it is unclear how this occurs. Since provincial education curricula do not include study of the Holocaust, Jewish life, or Jewish-Christian relations, the curricula cannot readily be credited with lowering prejudice. Because of the widespread use of the *Merchant of Venice* and *Oliver Twist* in the relatively early years, schooling may conceivably foster some degree of prejudice against Jews. Education may reduce prejudice because schools teach young people how to think and how to learn so that educated people learn to view Jews with objectivity in their early adult years. Another possibility is that many teachers hold democratic values and impart these democratic values to their students. That in Canada the better educated are less prejudiced is an important fact which should not be taken for granted.

Christianity and Anti-Jewish Prejudice

For the past 50 years, a growing community of Christian scholars of theology has written about the responsibility of the Christian churches for the existence of anti-Jewish prejudice. Some of the critical analysis has focussed on the content of Christian theology, for example on the idea that Jews are a deicide people bearing everlasting responsibility for their crime. Some of the critical analysis has emphasized the role of early church leaders in encouraging fratricidal attitudes. Other analysis has examined the leadership of Christian clergy in the anti-semitic political movements which emerged in Europe before World War II. Still other analysis has looked at the content of Christian liturgy and teachings (for a review of the literature treating Christianity as the principal cause of anti-Jewish prejudice, see Appendix D).

Rev. James Parkes, Professor Rosemary Ruether, Professor Alan Davies and other critics in Britain, the United States, and Canada have sought to influence the principles and practices of the Christian churches as well as the way in which the churches have understood their own histories. The critics have published a great deal and now receive a respectful hearing. But their view does not prevail.

The critics' viewpoint may not prevail because their viewpoint may be a misreading of Christian history or because, if valid, their view may be too disconcerting to be accepted. Whether or not it is a valid interpretation of Christian history, the critics' viewpoint does not seem to have much relevance for Canada in the 1980's. Even if we accept for purposes of argument that Christianity caused anti-Jewish hate in 5th or 15th century Europe or that the churches played an unfortunate role in Europe in the 1930's, it does not necessarily follow that Christianity is relevant to understanding anti-Jewish prejudice in Canada during the 1980's. In practice, Christianity's internal critics have done little research on the possible link between Christianity and anti-Jewish prejudice in contemporary North America.[10]

In place of systematic studies, there exist only snatchets of evidence about the possible link between Christianity and anti-Judaism in contemporary Canada. For example, in 1985 the Canadian Civil Liberties Association drew to public attention the use by the Separate School Board of Windsor of a teachers' manual which seems to encourage the transmission of anti-Jewish prejudice. For centuries, many Christian churches placed an emphasis on the passion of Jesus on the cross and, say the critics, the responsibility of all Jews for that act. Crucifixion was actually a Roman custom rather than a Jewish one. Furthermore, most Jews lived outside Israel, too far away to be aware of Jesus' existence. The Windsor Separate School Board's instructional manual reminds teachers of the responsibility of Jews and "all the people of Israel" for the crucifixion of Jesus and the imprisonment and maltreatment of his followers. In a section of seven pages, the teachers' manual mentions Jews or Israel seven times – six references to the alleged responsibility of Jews for the maltreatment of Jesus and his followers and one plea for Jews to convert. The teacher is asked to lead a classroom discussion in which the children are to be encouraged to contrast the faith and courage of Jesus and the apostles with the contrary-mindedness of the Jewish leaders and their alleged desire to censor and imprison the Christians.[11]

The content of the teachers' manual may constitute sufficient evidence to hypothesize that prejudice may be taught wherever the manual is used, but it is not sufficient evidence to demonstrate that prejudice is in fact taught. Without systematic research, it would be improper to rule out the possibility that teachers ignore the manual or that they make sure that their students learn to reject ancient Jews only and not contemporary Jews as well. It is possible that teachers convey the subject of the crucifixion according to their own feelings about Jews and Judaism rather than according to the requirements of the curriculum. Still another possibility is that children acquire their most fundamental feelings about Jews and the crucifixion from their parents rather than from their teachers.

If the Christian theological critics are right to claim that Christianity is at the heart of anti-Jewish prejudice, Christianity could contribute to anti-Jewish prejudice in Canada in one of four ways. *First*, the churches may play no active role in cultivating anti-Jewish prejudice today; instead, the seeds of prejudice may have been sown by a church of an earlier era. This possibility is an historical and philosophical question, which our book does not address.

Survey research can help pinpoint contemporary causes, but not historical ones.

Secondly, Christian dogma, liturgy, and teachings may cultivate anti-Jewish feelings today. According to this logic, religious Christians would be prejudiced against Jews while secular Christians would not. *Thirdly,* denominational differences may be paramount. Christian denominations have disagreed for centuries over many issues of dogma and interpretation, including responsibility for the crucifixion. If denominational differences are important, we should expect significant differences in attitudes towards Jews among members of different denominations. We might expect Protestants to be somewhat less prejudiced because Protestant denominations have been more quick to modernize their dogma and ritual to take into consideration modern democratic ideas. Furthermore, Protestants have placed a greater emphasis on the Old Testament and may therefore have more positive feelings about ancient Jews and their spiritual heirs. Because of their church's stronger ties to Christian history and tradition, we might expect Roman Catholics to display a higher incidence of prejudice against Jews. *Fourthly,* ethnic culture may matter more than religious dogma or denominational identity. For example, we might expect French Canadians to be more prejudiced than English Canadians because French Canada modernized more recently. Ontario had a government department responsible for education early in the century. In Quebec, responsibility for education did not leave the hands of the church until the Quiet Revolution of 1960.

Religiosity and Prejudice

American social researchers in the 1960's found evidence that religiosity predicted anti-Jewish prejudice, that people who believed in the old verities were more apt to dislike the Jews of antiquity as well as the Jews of today.[12] Both the American survey and our own asked people if they thought that it was necessary to believe in Jesus to go to heaven. The Americans found that respondents who agreed that such a belief was necessary were apt to be prejudiced against Jews. In view of the declining dogmatism of the Christian churches as well as an apparent decline in the anti-Jewish content of liturgy and doctrine, we might expect no such relationship to emerge in Canada. In fact, we found no relationship across the sample of Canadians between their view about the necessity of Christian belief for admission to heaven and their attitudes to Judaism. Among Canadians as a whole, *people who believed in the necessity of Christian commitment for salvation were not more apt to be anti-Jewish.*[13] It is an important and hopeful finding from our survey data that devotion to Christianity and prejudice against Jews were unrelated.

Once again following the leadership of the American study, we examined the impact of religious tolerance on anti-Judaism. Respondents were asked whether they agreed or disagreed with the statement that "*Missionaries from Non-Christian religions should NOT have the same right to spread their teachings as Christian missionaries.*" In the American study, people opposed to equal rights for non-Christian missionaries tended to be prejudiced against Jews. Among Canadians as a whole, we found such a pattern, but only a very modest pattern. For example, the number of people who thought that Jews have too much power or who do not know if they have too much power was 38% among people favouring equal rights for non-Christian missionaries and 48% among those opposed to equal rights.

Denomination, Language, and Prejudice

While the opinion data did not yield differences between the devout and the secular, the data showed differences among denominations and between English and French Canada. Roman Catholics were more prejudiced than Protestants as a whole. The number of Catholics who thought that Jews have too much power was twice the number among Protestants (22% vs. 11%). Roman Catholics were more apt to consider an exaggeration the estimate of six million casualties from the Holocaust. Twice as many Catholics as Protestants considered the estimate to be inflated (21% vs. 11%). Catholics were not more likely than Protestants to actually blame Jews for the Holocaust (18% vs. 18%). It is not clear why Catholics were no more likely to blame Jews for the Holocaust. One possibility is that the Catholic respondents were not in fact more prejudiced against Jews in a Holocaust context. Another possibility is that Catholics are normally less judgemental and less inclined to assign blame than Protestants.

Although it is statistically true that Catholics were twice as likely to believe that Jews are too powerful and twice as likely to doubt the official estimate of Holocaust casualties, is Catholicism the actual cause of anti-Jewish feeling? Solving this puzzle is as much a philosophical task as a statistical or factual one. The data showed French-speaking Catholics to be more prejudiced against Jews than their English-speaking co-religionists. For example, as many as 23% of francophones said that Jews have too much power as compared to 18% of English-speaking Catholics and 11% of Protestants. One can argue that French Canadians are prejudiced at least in part because of their culture rather than solely because of their religion.

Furthermore, many English-speaking Catholics are first, second, or third generation Canadians with origins in European countries having pronounced anti-Jewish as well as despotic traditions. One can therefore argue that even English-speaking Catholics are more anti-Jewish than Protestants as a result of their different national origins. One can argue that Anglicans and other Protestants are relatively free of anti-Jewish phobias because Protestantism and democracy are closely intertwined. The Church of England (Anglicanism in Canada) is not merely a Christian sect; it is also the national church and hence the embodiment of national culture of England, the world's oldest parliamentary democracy.

Deciding whether Catholics are essentially or accidentally more anti-Jewish may be an unsolvable problem. The potential counter-arguments are endless. For example, one could say that the fact that Protestant countries are more apt to be democratic is not accidental but intrinsic to the religion. Protestant countries tend to be more democratic and tolerant because the Protestant churches were never as well organized, as centrally controlled, and as interested in power as the Catholic church. One can argue that French Canadian culture and Roman Catholicism have always been inseparable so that it is improper to attribute anti-Jewish prejudice to the culture rather than the religion of French Canada.

From a moral or ethical perspective, it is not actually necessary to know if the greater anti-Jewish prejudice of French Canada is caused by Catholicism. From a moral perspective, it is sufficient to know that anti-Judaism is a more serious problem in French Canada and that in French Canada the power to reteach is in the hands of Catholicism rather than Protestantism.

Among the Protestant denominations, anti-Jewish prejudice is especially concentrated among the small group of Presbyterians. Perhaps on account of their heritage of Calvinist judgementalism, Presbyterians were most prepared to blame the Holocaust on its victims. Only the Presbyterians were more apt to blame Jews than the French Catholics. An extraordinary one out of four Presbyterians took this position. Almost as many Presbyterians as English Catholics declared that Jews are too powerful. Presbyterians were as apt to deny that six million died as the English Catholics. In the particular case of Presbyterians, anti-Judaism was accompanied by an unwillingness to grant equal rights to non-Christian missionaries. As many as 62% of Presbyterians opposed equals rights as compared to 21% among members of the United Church and 14% among the Baptists. Furthermore, in the particular case of Presbyterians, general religious intolerance did predict anti-Judaism. For example, among those Presbyterians who opposed equal rights for non-Christian missionaries, an extraordinary 80% thought that Jews are too powerful. Tolerance for non-Christian missionaries did not predict attitudes to Jews among members of other denominations.

Among the Protestant groups, Lutherans, Anglicans, and "Other Protestants" were least likely to be prejudiced. Only 3% of Lutherans thought that Jews are too powerful. The low apparent prejudice among Canadian Lutherans may surprise readers familiar with Martin Luther's profound racism or with the well documented enthusiasm of German Lutheran Pastors for the Nazi movement. On the other hand, the mainstream Lutheran denomination has gone on record as repudiating Luther's own anti-Judaism. Lutheran liturgy seems relatively free of anti-Jewish content. Most Lutherans in Canada are Canadian-born and probably of Scandinavian origin. There is also a possibility that our sample of Lutheran respondents did not reflect well Lutherans at large. Our Lutheran sample was smaller and therefore less reliable than larger denominations such as Catholics.

Anti-Jewish Prejudice in French Canada

Anti-Jewish sentiment is a problem of profound significance in French Canada. Fig. 6.3 shows that as many as two out of five francophones chose at least one hostile answer among the three measures of prejudice. As many as 39% of French-speaking respondents were prepared to say that Jews have too much power or that Jews caused the Holocaust or that six million did not perish. This is twice the rate among English Canadian respondents. The rate of acknowledged ignorance was about the same in the two language groups.

Among certain sectors of French Canada, anti-Jewish prejudice is a majority view. Fig. 6.4 shows that only 15% of Canadians as a whole believed that Jews are too powerful. This figure rose to 20% among residents of Quebec and New Brunswick, 26% among Catholics in these two provinces, 31% among French Catholics in the two provinces, and 40% among French Catholics with low education. Among poorly educated males with limited exposure to the media, a majority expressed profoundly prejudiced views. The prejudiced views of French Canadians have implications for the future of minority-majority relations within Quebec. The prejudices of French Canadians also have implications for the conduct of democracy. When a large segment of society suffers from ethnic or religious prejudice, the society is susceptible to the appeals of unscrupulous and potentially despotic politicians. This is one of the reasons why the intensity of anti-Jewish prejudice in a given society is sometimes said to be a litmus test of the health of its democratic political life.[14]

Fig 6.3
PREJUDICE AND ADMITTED IGNORANCE
AMONG ENGLISH AND FRENCH

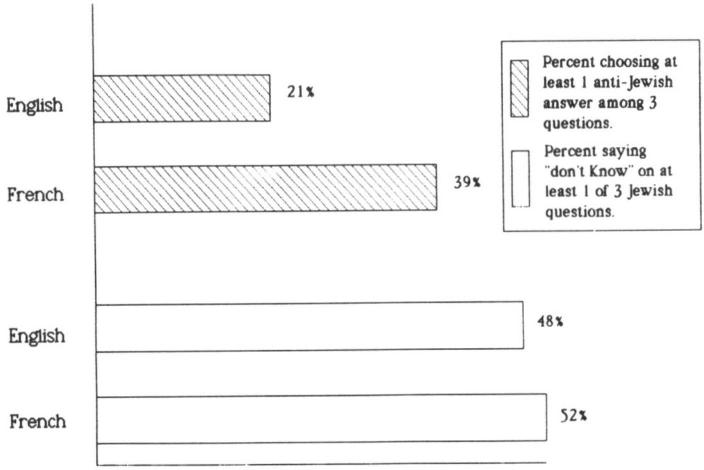

Interpretation: English and French Canadians did not differ in their willingness to say that they "don't know" in answer to questions about blame for the Holocaust, Jewish power, and the number who perished. But, Francophones were twice as likely to choose prejudiced answers.

Fig 6.4

A PATTERN OF RISING ANTI-JEWISH PREJUDICE

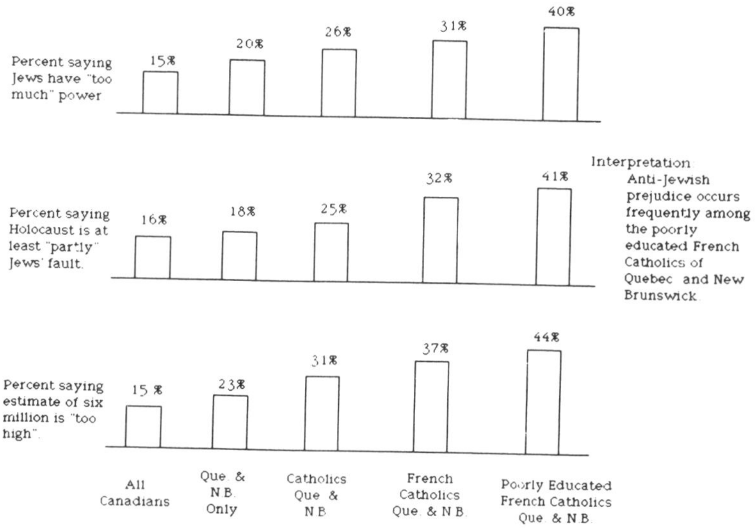

The paragraphs which follow are offered as illustrations of the historical antecedents of the anti-Jewish prejudice in French Canada found in our survey data. The phenomena described below are not presented as evidence of anti-Jewish prejudice in French Canada. Our evidence of anti-Jewish prejudice in French Canada is based on the public opinion data. Readers interested in systematic evidence of anti-Jewish prejudice in the French Canadian past can turn to historical and literary scholarship.[15]

The historical antecedents of French Canadian prejudice are traceable in the hostility of the French Canadian clergy. During the 19th century, the clerical forces were the ones most apt to oppose the right of individual Jews, if elected, to hold a seat in the legislature. In the early 1930's, before Hitler could deploy the resources of the German state to spread anti-Jewish hate around the world, anti-Jewish movements were strong in Quebec. The francophone clergy sought to abolish Jewish advisory committees on education and to strip Jews of Canadian citizenship. Quebec's leading Nazi, Adrien Arcand, became the first publicist for Maurice Duplessis's long governing National Union party, whose press published anti-Judaica along with party literature. In 1934, the first Jewish intern in a Catholic hospital resigned and emigrated to the United States after the interns in six Catholic hospitals went on strike and the nursing staff threatened to follow suit.

The *Protocols of the Elders of Zion* achieved considerable exposure, either in the original or in the ideas disseminated by parochial newsletters and the ordinary press. In 1937, two years before the outbreak of World War II, a parish paper observed:

> All countries are unanimous in recognizing that we have no greater enemy than the Jews. They are the source of all great cataclysms. They participated in the French Revolution and the Russian Revolution. They are the most fervent leaders of Freemasonry, the promoters of discord, the agitators of strikes, and finally they are the propagandists of Communism.[16]

The newspaper *Le Devoir,* influential then as now, disseminated anti-Jewish prejudice. In 1937, the editor of the paper carried a special editorial entitled "Anti-Semitism, Growing Peril" The editorial conveyed the medieval theological concern that Jews refuse to convert (i.e. assimilate) and the modern fear that Jews manipulate the planet:

> What above all worries non-Jews is the feeling of harbouring portions of another people, who are unassimilable, from a nation which aims at the domination of the world and of whom several members foment revolutions . . .[17]

In 1978, author Victor Téboul published a remarkable book tracing the persistence of anti-Jewish themes in French Canadian literature.[18] In *Mondes*

Chimeriques, a novel appearing in 1944, the author has a character who is a tormented half-Jew bemoan the fact that ownership of material possessions is a "juste" punishment inflicted on Israelites for the crucifixion.[19] In another novel of the period, a French Canadian named Bédard changes his name to Bédarovitch, adding a suffix which sounds Jewish to the French Canadian ear in order to succeed in business.[20] In the 1970 novel *Il Est Par La*, popular author Roch Carrier includes the observation that ". . . Jews control the police, governments, and business; the whole world knows that Jews control even the English."[21] In his overview of French Canadian literature, Victor Téboul shows that prejudice invades even works of reference. Thus, the 1955 Bélisle dictionary defines as a Jew "one who lends usuriously or who sells for an exhorbitantly expensive price, or, in general anyone who tries to earn money harshly."[22]

The theme of a satanic Jewish influence persists in the French Canadian literature of the 1980's. In the popular novel-cum-movie, *Le Matou* (the tomcat), the villainous character is named Egon Ratablavsky. Ratablavsky has an ending which, in a Quebec context, sounds Eastern European and/or Jewish. Set in a district of Montreal where francophones and Jews were once neighbours, *Le Matou* tells the story of a francophone restauranteur threatened by Ratablavsky's diabolical machinations. Ratablavsky portrays himself alternatively as a Czech, a Polish Jew, a Nazi agent, and a rural Québecois. We lack survey data to indicate whether French Canadians today would see the villain as essentially a Jewish figure. During the middle ages, Europeans would have had little difficulty recognizing Ratablavsky as a classic satanic-Jewish figure, appearing deviously under many guises.

The satanic-Jewish figure appears in an undisguised form in a recent French language school book on Acadian culture. A compendium of the "18 most beautiful legends," the book tells the story of the "wandering Jew." Because the Jew mistreated Jesus and refused to help him carry the cross, he is condemned to wander the earth in misery until the end of time. He is not even allowed to die. "Bad like the devil," he "looks like the devil." He "gathers up children and makes them die." In 1985, the New Brunswick Ministry of Education ceased authorizing the book's use in the province's schools.[23]

Ethnic Contact

People's attitudes towards ethnic groups can be influenced by their religious education, by their secular education, by the ethnic group to which they belong, and also by their personal experiences. Chapter 5 showed that Canadians who had met at least one Jew were less apt to be prejudiced. In view of this link between personal contact and lower prejudice, it is important to know the pattern of ethnic contact among Canadians.

Table 6.2
Contact with Ethnic Groups among Anglophones and Francophones

	% No Contact at all	
Contact with	**Among francophones**	**Among anglophones**
Italians	53	29
Jews	68	34
Blacks	53	28
Asians	66	35
Germans	69	26
Scots	61	20
Average	62	29

Interpretation: Francophones have much less contact with members of all ethnic groups than do anglophones.

Table 6.2 shows that number of English and French speaking Canadians who report no contact with members of each of the six ethnic groups examined in this study. The table reveals a slight tendency for Canadians – anglophone or francophone – to have less contact with Jews than with members of most of the other groups. But, the differences are not major. The most important finding is that francophones have appreciably less contact with members of the six ethnic groups than do anglophones. Among anglophones, only a minority – one-third and sometimes much less – acknowledge never having met members of one or other of these ethnic groups. Only 20% of anglophones say that they have never met a Scot and only 34% say that they have never met a Jew.

The number of French Canadians isolated from contact with these ethnic minorities is more than twice as high. More than half of French Canadians admit to never having met an Italian or Black. More than two-thirds say that they have never met a Jew. The social isolation of French Canadians may go part way to explain their intense levels of prejudice. However, social isolation cannot be used to explain the special tendency of francophones to be prejudiced against Jews because francophones are no more isolated from Jews than from Asians and Germans and hardly more isolated than from Scots.

Nonetheless, in the particular case of French Canadians, personal contact with a Jew may reduce the magnitude of negative feeling. We did not ask respondents to indicate the context in which they had contact with a Jew – whether it was in business, in a university classroom, in a private home or at a cafe. Whatever the context, prejudice seems to have been reduced by contact. Fig. 6.5 shows that francophones who have had at least some contact with a Jew were half as likely to say that Jews have too much power in Canadian society or to say that they did not know whether Jews have too much power. Among francophones having some contact with Jews, the proportion blaming the Holocaust on Jews or not knowing whether to blame it on Jews was only 29% as compared to 53% among francophones who had never met a Jew.

Fig 6.5

ANTI-JUDAISM AND ADMITTED IGNORANCE AMONG FRANCOPHONES WITH OR WITHOUT JEWISH CONTACT.

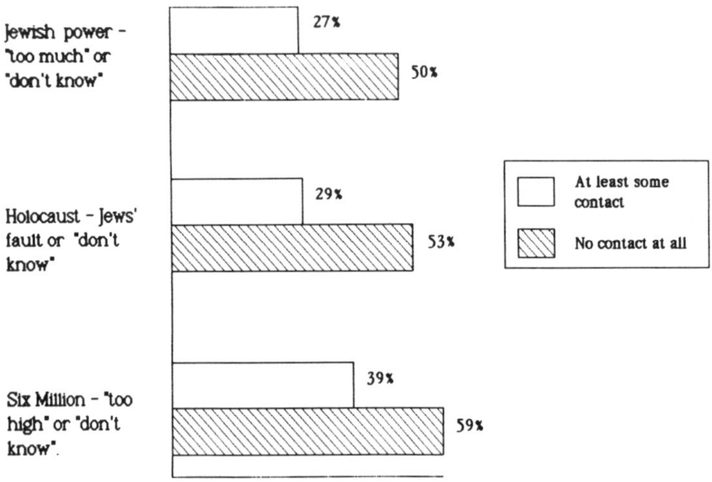

Interpretation: Among Francophones, those who have at least minimal contact with Jews are noticeably less likely to choose prejudiced or "don't know" answers.

We do not know why personal contact is so effective in reducing hostility among French Canadians. One possibility is that the decline in prejudice is greater among francophones than among anglophones because proportionately more francophones are prejudiced at the outset. Another possibility is that personal contact may have a different and stronger meaning in French than in English Canada.

Rural francophones were no more or less anti-Jewish than urban francophones with one exception. The same proportions of rural and urban francophones said that Jews were too powerful and the same proportions blamed Jews for the Holocaust. But, rural francophones were more apt to doubt that six million Jews were killed. French-speaking scholars have sometimes attributed anti-Jewish prejudice among francophones to the presence in past decades of Jewish shopkeepers on the St. Lawrence Boulevard strip which historically separated English from French Montreal. The fact that the only Jews known to francophones were merchants, it is said, aroused the animosity of the French.[24] If this were an adequate explanation of French anti-Judaism, we should find that rural French-speakers are less hostile than urban French-speakers and that contact with Jews breeds prejudice. The data show the opposite. Rural francophones were no less hostile while personal contact reduced prejudice.

Anti-Jewish and Anti-Ethnic Prejudice

The last remaining question to consider is how anti-Jewish and anti-ethnic prejudice are related. Chapter 5 showed that people who were anti-Jewish tended to be anti-Black, anti-Asian, anti-Italian and so forth but that anti-Jewish sentiment also had a life of its own. We examined patterns of prejudice towards different ethnic groups among religious groups and the two linguistic communities in Canada. The Protestant denominations did not differ among themselves with the notable exception of Presbyterians. English-speaking and French-speaking Catholics displayed different patterns of prejudice.

Fig. 6.6 and table 6.3 compare the levels of prejudice among Presbyterians, English Catholics, French Catholics, and Protestants as a whole towards the six different ethnic groups. The item used to measure prejudice was the question about power in Canadian society. Protestants as a whole were the least prejudiced group, but Presbyterians were appreciably more prejudiced than either English or French Catholics. As many as 16% of Presbyterians thought that each of the six groups on average had too much power as compared to 14% among French Catholics, 13% among English Catholics, and 9% among all Protestants combined.

Fig 6.6

ETHNIC PREJUDICE AMONG PROTESTANTS, ENGLISH CATHOLICS, FRENCH CATHOLICS AND PRESBYTERIANS

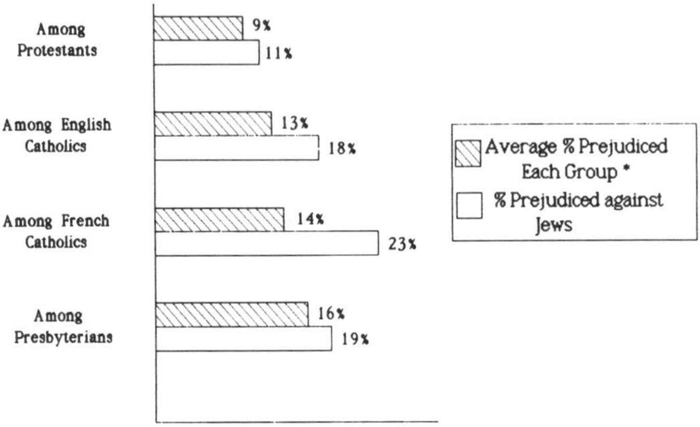

* Average percent saying that each of 6 ethnic groups has "too much power".

Interpretation: (1) Presbyterians and French Catholics were generally more prejudiced than non-Presbyterian Protestants.
(2) Catholics, especially Francophones, were particularly prejudiced against Jews.

Table 6.3
Ethnic Prejudice among Four Groups (% saying "too much" power) among

Power of	Presbyterians	Fr. R.C's	Eng. R.C.'s	Protestants
Italians	25	18	15	12
Jews	19	23	18	11
Blacks	8	10	10	6
Asians	8	13	14	9
Germans	21	11	11	4
Scots	17	10	8	4
Average	16	14	13	9

Interpretation: (1) Catholics and Presbyterians tend to be more prejudiced than Protestants. (2) Catholics, especially francophones, tend to target Jews while Protestants, especially Presbyterians, tend to target Italians.

Jews and Italians were the most apt to be the object of prejudice but they were rejected by different groups. The Presbyterians clearly singled out Italians. Fully 25% declared that Italians have too much power in Canadian society – a remarkable figure considering the almost complete absence of Italians from the higher public service, cabinets, the banks, major industry, and the media. Italian Canadians do earn high incomes, mainly as a result of their high representation in the well paid construction industry. But, Italians are absent from most of those positions which objective observors would normally describe as powerful. Italians are also singled out by Protestants as a whole although Protestants generally do not express the same intensity of prejudice as Presbyterians. The animosity of Presbyterians and of Protestants may stem from age-old Protestant-Catholic theological rivalries. In Protestant Europe, the words "Machiavelli" and "Italian" were often used as symbols of the alleged immorality, corruption, and byzantine character of the Vatican and the Italian world in which it functioned.

It is more difficult to account for the animosity of French and English Catholics towards Italians. French Catholics may be prejudiced as a result of disappointment that so many Italians chose to assimilate to English rather than French Canada. English Catholics may be anti-Italian for the same reason that they are less anti-Jewish than French Catholics – they have been influenced by the outlook of the predominantly Protestant society in which they live.

While Italians are the main targets of Protestants and especially Presbyterians, Jews are the main targets of Roman Catholics. As many as 18% of English Catholics and 23% of French Catholics declared that Jews are too powerful in Canadian society. No group was singled out for special attention as much as Jews were by French Catholics. In English-speaking Canada, the preoccupation of Catholics with Jews was also high, although its intensity was exceeded slightly by the preoccupation of Presbyterians with Italians. The special interest of Catholics in Jews is especially noteworthy given the general tolerance of Catholics. In contrast to Presbyterians, Catholics were apt to say that non-Christian missionaries should have the same right to preach their message as Christian missionaries. It looks as if age-old theological battles never die.

* * * * *

Ignoring the Zundel affair, the chapter looked in some detail at the kinds of Canadians who are apt to be prejudiced against Jews. The least hostile person was apt to be an English-speaking, university educated woman who belonged to a Protestant congregation other than the Presbyterian Church and who was in her 40's. The most hostile person was apt to be a French-speaking, Roman Catholic, poorly educated male resident of Quebec or New Brunswick.

Older people were apt to be prejudiced for obvious reasons; they grew up in more prejudiced times. Younger people – those under 25 – may have been prejudiced against Jews in a Holocaust context for reasons of ignorance and/or as a result of the curricular failures of Canada's educational system.

Although women were as prejudiced against the other groups as men, they were noticeably less hostile towards Jews, especially women with higher education. We have no ready explanation.

Our data showed that intensity of Christian religious commitment is not a source of anti-Jewish feeling as it was a generation ago in the United States. In Canada, strong Christian believers were no more hostile than others. Presbyterians, French Catholics and English Catholics were appreciably more prejudiced against Jews than Protestants as a whole. On the basis of our inevitably small sample of Presbyterians, it seemed as if Presbyterian anti-Judaism belonged to a larger pattern of ethnic hostility and religious intolerance. Catholics were not especially prejudiced against different groups and not especially intolerant of non-Christian missionary rights. But, Catholics displayed a tendency to be especially prejudiced against Jews.

1 Several recent books have documented the role of young people, especially male university students, in revolutionary movements. See, for example, *Who Voted for Hitler?* (Princeton: Princeton University Press, 1982) by the McGill political sociologist, Richard Hamilton.

2 See Lita-Rose Betcherman, *The Swastika and the Maple Leaf* (Toronto: Fitzhenry and Whiteside, 1975) for a review of this period.

3 *ibid.*

4 *ibid.*

5 Irving Abella and Harold Troper, *None Is Too Many: Canada and the Jews of Europe, 1933-1948* (Toronto: Lester & Orpen Denys, 1982).

6 Conrad Winn and John McMenemy, *Political Parties in Canada* (Toronto: McGraw Hill Ryerson, 1976), chap. 7

7 Personal communication from Professor Aviva Freedman, Chair, Linguistics Department, Carleton University, summer, 1985.

8 We consulted several specialists in feminist research and ethnic prejudice, but they were either at a loss to account for the finding or offered explanations which contradicted those offered by others. Special thanks to Professors Jill Vickers, Elinor Burwell, Daivak Stasiulis, and Francis Henry of Carleton and York Universities.

9 Statistically minded readers may note that the only significant difference between male and female perceptions of power (at the 0.5 level) involved perceptions of Jewish power.

10 See Alan Davies, *Anti-semitism and the Christian Mind: the Crisis of Conscience after Auschwitz* (Toronto, 1969).

11 pp. 36-42 of the French language teachers' manual employed by the Separate School Board of Windsor. Our appreciation to Marie Moliner of the Canadian Civil Liberties Association, Toronto, for providing this material.

12 Charles Y. Glock and Rodney Stark, *Christian Beliefs and Anti-Semitism: a Scientific Study of the Ways in Which the Teachings of Christian Churches Shape American Attitudes towards the Jews* (New York: Harper and Row, 1966).

13 For a recent argument that intense Christian commitment and anti-Jewish prejudice may not be related today, see Richard John Neuhaus, "What the Fundamentalists Want," *Commentary* (May, 1985).

14 James Parkes has referred to anti-Jewish prejudice in this vein.

15 See Horace Minor, *St. Denis* (Chicago: University of Chicago Press, 1939), E.C. Hughes, *French Canada in Transition* (Chicago: University of Chicago Press, 1943), A.J. Bélanger, *L'Apoliticisme des Ideologies Québecoises* (Ste. Foy: Les Presse de l'Université Laval, 1974), F. Dumont *et al.*, *Idéologies au Canada Francais, 1850-1900* and *1900-1929* (Ste. Foy: Les Presses de l'Université Laval, 1971 and 1973), R. Jones, *L'Idéologie de l'Action Catholique* (Ste. Foy: Les Presses de l'Université Laval, 1974), Lita-Rose Betcherman, *The Swastika and the Maple Leaf* (Toronto: Fitzhenry and Whiteside, 1978) and Victor Téboul, *Mythe et Images du Juif au Québec* (Montreal: Editions de Lagrave, 1978). For a social science study, see Werner Cohn, "English and French Canadian Public Opinion on Jews and Israel: Some Poll Data," *Canadian Ethnic Studies* (1979), 31-48.

[16] Quoted in Lita-Rose Betcherman, *The Swastika and the Maple Leaf* (Toronto: Fitzhenry and Whiteside, 1075), p. 92

[17] *ibid.*, p. 92.

[18] *Mythe et Image du Juif au Québec* (Montreal: Editions de Lagrave, 1978).

[19] Quoted in Téboul from Francois Hertel, *Mondes Chimeriques* (Montreal: Editions Pascal, 1944), p. 75

[20] In Téboul, from Roger Lemelin, *Au Pied de la Pente Douce* (Montreal: Le Cercle du Livre de France, 1967), p. 30

[21] Quoted by Téboul, p. 25. Our translation from the French.

[22] *Dictionnaire Belisle de la Language Francaise du Canada* (Montreal: Société des Editions Lelond Limitée, 1955), p. 680. Our translation from the French.

[23] *Les Plus Belles Légendes Acadiennes* (Montréal: Stanké, 1983).

[24] In a marxist analysis, Denis Moniere points to envy and economic competition between French and Jewish small businessmen. See his *Le Développement des Idéologies au Québec* (Montreal: Editions Québec/Amérique, 1977).

Chapter 7

Conclusion

Newspaper columnists, civil libertarians, and various experts alerted us to the importance of the Zundel trial. With few exceptions, most experts who expressed a view on the question declared that the trial was un-necessary and potentially harmful. The trial merely gave an evil person and an evil movement a platform for racist and Nazi rhetoric. Many Canadians, it was said, would become susceptible to Holocaust denial propaganda.

Our national public opinion data tell a different story. The trial did not engender support for Zundel's viewpoint. A major reason why Ernst Zundel failed to augment his following is that the people most receptive to his arguments were least aware that he was even on trial. The survey data show anti-Jewish prejudice to be strongest among those who were poorly educated, who were ill-informed, and who did not use the media to follow the news.

Among Canadians who were free of prejudice at the outset, the trial appears to have increased knowledge of the Holocaust and to have intensified sympathy for Jews, according to the testimony of the respondents themselves. The trial seems to have reduced prejudices against Jews in a European context but not to have affected prejudices against Jews as they are perceived in a Canadian context.

Increased public understanding of the Holocaust and increased sympathy for Jews were accompanied by a tendency to believe that other people now have doubts about the Holocaust. Paradoxically, objective public opinion has improved while subjective public opinion, the "climate" of opinion, has worsened. Canadians have become more knowledgeable and more benign while fearing that their fellow citizens have become less knowledgeable and less benign. The mass media played an important role in educating Canadians about the Holocaust and also in leading Canadians to believe that the trial had caused more of their fellow citizens to have doubts about the official record of this chapter in history.

For the short-term, it is a positive development that unprejudiced Canadians became better informed about the Holocaust and more sympathetic to Jews. However, for the long-term it is potentially dangerous that Canadians who followed the trial seemed to perceive their neighbours as less sympathetic to Jews than they themselves felt. Among Canadians reporting a change of sympathy towards Jews, the vast majority said that they had become more sympathetic rather than less sympathetic. If the large sympathetic group were to perceive itself as a group under siege over an extended period of time, the size of this group might dwindle as its members hesitate to voice their opinions.

Individual newspapers or broadcasters may have provided inadequate or unsatisfactory reporting on the trial and/or the Holocaust, as some critics have suggested. Our data offer little evidence in support of the view that the media as a whole or one medium as opposed to the other exercised a negative influence on public opinion. Because of the nature of the medium and the nature of its audience, television exercised a particularly strong impact on the attitudes of Canadians. Followers of television news were especially apt to report increased sympathy for Jews. Television succeeded in informing people about elementary facts such as how many people perished but it did not succeed in explaining how and why the Holocaust took place. Heavy consumers of television news were no more apt to understand who was responsible than light consumers of news.

The differences in the coverage provided by the English and French media paralleled the differences in the attitudes of English and French Canadians towards Jews. The English press and television provided much more coverage of the trial and much more coverage of the Holocaust outside the context of the trial. The English media (except for Newfoundland) provided extensive coverage of nonviolent Jewish events (eg. a story on novelist I.B. Singer) while the French media provided essentially no such coverage. Jews in French news were portrayed almost exclusively in the context of victimization.

Anti-Jewish prejudice and admitted ignorance of Jewish issues are serious problems in Canada, and were serious problems before the trial of Ernst Zundel. On the positive side, large numbers of Canadians were knowledgeable and unprejudiced in the Western provinces, especially British Columbia. University graduates, especially women, were almost devoid of prejudice. Christian believers were no more apt to be prejudiced against Jews than nonbelievers. People in their forties were less prejudiced than the older generations.

On the negative side, young people were strikingly ignorant of the Holocaust and were twice as inclined as people in their middle years to blame

Jews for their own victimization. The attitudes of the young call out for Holocaust curricula in the schools and a careful look at how Jews and Judaism are portrayed in assigned readings.

On the negative side, Roman Catholics, especially francophones, were apt to be prejudiced against Jews. Among poorly educated male Roman Catholic francophones in Quebec or New Brunswick, the number who were prejudiced against Jews rose to approximately half the general population. Protestants also exhibited prejudice against Jews, particularly Presbyterians. Among Catholics, prejudice against Jews tended to be more focussed.

French Canada represents opportunities. According to our data, francophones revealed a remarkable ability to jettison prejudice once they encountered their first Jew. It may not be possible for every French Canadian to personally meet a Jew. But, the French press and television offer marvellous opportunities to transmit information about Jewish religious, cultural, and secular life. Unlike their English counterparts, the French newspapers and Radio-Canada television carry almost no information on Jews outside a context of victimization. The exclusive portrayal of Jews as victims may do little to reduce prejudice. The victimization of Jews is after all ordained by medieval Christian theology as punishment for deicide. However, the sustained coverage of nonviolent Jewish events by the French media could do much to open minds.

Appendix A

Design Of The Sample (as supplied by Gallup)

The Omnibus maintains a modified probability sample in all centres over 1,000 in population. A quota sample is used in rural farm and rural non-farm centres. An independent sample of individuals is selected for each survey.

The sampling procedure is designed to produce an approximation of the adult civilian population, 18 years and older, living in Canada, except for those persons in institutions such as prisons or hospitals, or those residing in Labrador, the Yukon or the Northwest Territories. Survey data can be applied to this population for the purpose of projecting pecentages into numbers of people.

The sample design incorporates statification by six community size groups, based on the 1981 Census data: Cities of 500,000 population and over, those between 100,000 and 500,000, 30,000 to 100,000, 10,000 to 30,000, 1,000 to 10,000 and rural farm and rural non-farm areas.

The population is arrayed in geographic order by community size and within those classifications, by census enumeration areas. Enumeration areas, on the average, contain about 500 to 1,000 people.

A total of 105 enumeration areas are selected randomly from this array. Within urban centres, a random block sampling procedure is used to select starting points for interviewers. The interviewer is provided with a map of the enumeration area, showing the location of the starting point and is required to follow a specified route in the selection of households. Within the household, the youngest male, 18 years and over, at home at the time of the interview, is questioned. If there is no male available, or when the male quota is completed, the youngest available female, 18 years and over is interviewed.

The selection of rural farm and rural non-farm interviewing locations follows the sample design established for urban centres in terms of geographic dispersion and random selection of enumeration areas. Because of the low population density and wide dispersion of households, the random block sampling procedure is replaced by quota sampling based on sex and age.

The design of this sample has been based on population statistics of the Census of Canada, 1981.

Sample Characteristics

	Number	Percent
National	1054	100
Region:		
Atlantic	100	9
Quebec	268	25
Ontario	377	36
Prairies	189	18
B.C.	120	11
Age:		
18 - 29 years	325	31
30 - 49 years	372	35
50 years and over	343	33
Did not state	14	1
Sex:		
Male	515	49
Female	539	51
Education:		
Elementary School	165	16
High School	682	65
University	201	19
Did not state	6	1
Income:		
Under $10,000	110	10
$10,000 - $19,999	188	18
$20,000 - $29,999	182	17
$30,000 and over	359	34
Did not state	215	20
Mother Tongue:		
English	639	61

French	283	27
Other	127	12
Did not state	5	*
Community Size:		
Over 100,000	579	55
10,000 - 1,000	149	14
Under 10,000	326	31

Note: Percentages may not add exactly to 100 due to rounding.

* Less than 0.5 percentage points.

Appendix B

The Questionnaire

INTERVIEWER DON'T READ ALOUD WORDS IN CAPITAL LETTERS/CIRCLE APPROPRIATE NUMBERS OR CHECK BOXES

SUGGESTED INTRODUCTION

Good day. I'm from the Gallup Organization, and I'd like to talk to you about a few topics on national public opinion and on marketing.

SECTION A . . . ASK EVERYONE

1. Turning for a moment to religious matters:

   Do you think that it is necessary for a person to believe in Jesus Christ to go to Heaven.
   Would you say this is: READ ALOUD.

   Completely true? 1
   Probably true? 2
   Probably not true? 3
   Definitely not true? 4

   DON'T KNOW 5

---

2. I'm going to read you a statement.

   'Missionaries from Non-Christian religions should **not** have the same right to spread their teachings as Christian Missionaries'. Do you agree or disagree with that statement?

AGREE - SHOULD NOT	1
DISAGREE - SHOULD	2
DON'T KNOW	3

3. Do you have contact with any member of these ethnic groups? ROTATE ORDER STARTING WITH (✓). **HAND CARD 1**

   First, the . . . do you often, occasionally, rarely or never have contact with . . .?

   What about the . . . (READ QUESTION FOR EACH ETHNIC GROUP).

	OFTEN	**OCCASIONALLY**	**RARELY**	**NEVER**
ITALIANS	1	2	3	4
✓JEWS	1	2	3	4
BLACKS	1	2	3	4
ASIANS	1	2	3	4
GERMANS	1	2	3	4
SCOTTISH/SCOTS	1	2	3	4

4. Would you say that members of the following ethnic groups have too much, just enough, or not enough power in Canada? READ EACH ETHNIC GROUP — ROTATE ORDER STARTING WITH (✓) **HAND CARD 1**

	TOO MUCH POWER	**JUST ENOUGH POWER**	**NOT ENOUGH POWER**	**DON'T KNOW**
ITALIANS	1	2	3	4
✓JEWS	1	2	3	4
BLACKS	1	2	3	4
ASIANS	1	2	3	4
GERMANS	1	2	3	4
SCOTTISH/SCOTS	1	2	3	4

SECTION B . . . ASK EVERYONE

1. The media have talked a lot about the recent court trial in Toronto of Ernst Zundel. Do you happen to know what Ernst Zundel was convicted of? DO NOT READ ALOUD.

CAUSING HARM TO RACIAL/SOCIAL HARMONY; DISTRIBUTING HATE LITERATURE; CLAIMING HOLOCAUST A JEWISH HOAX; ANTI-SEMITIC LITERATURE; PROMOTING HATRED TOWARDS JEWS, ETC. 1

OTHER (SPECIFY) . . . .

. . . . 2

DON'T KNOW 3

---

2. Thinking back to the treatment of the Jews in Europe, before and during World II, do you think the persecution of the Jews was . . . READ STATEMENTS ALOUD

Mostly the fault of the Jews 1
Partly the fault of the Jews 2
Not at all the fault of the Jews 3

DON'T KNOW 4

---

3. According to official estimates, about six million Jews were killed in the Holocaust. Do you think this estimate is too high, about right, or too low?

TOO HIGH 1
ABOUT RIGHT 2
TOO LOW 3

DON'T KNOW 4

---

4. Has the Zundel trial made you feel more sympathetic or less sympathetic towards the Jews?

MORE SYMPATHETIC 1
LESS SYMPATHETIC 2
SAME/WAS NOT AFFECTED (VOLUNTEERED) 3

DON'T KNOW 4

---

5. Has the Zundel trial made you feel more sympathetic, or less sympathetic towards the Germans?

MORE SYMPATHETIC 1
LESS SYMPATHETIC 2
SAME/WAS NOT AFFECTED (VOLUNTEERED) 3

DON'T KNOW 4

---

6. The media have talked a lot about the doubts and questions raised by Mr. Zundel over the past few weeks.

   In your opinion, are there a few Canadians, many Canadians, or almost no Canadians who now believe we should seriously question the historical records of this period?

   A FEW 1
   MANY 2
   ALMOST NONE 3

   DON'T KNOW 4

---

7. How many times over the past 7 days have you . . .

   a. watched news broadcsts on TV?

   0 1 2 3 4 5 6 7 OR MORE

   b. read news reports in the newspaper?

   0 1 2 3 4 5 6 7 OR MORE

SECTION C . . . ASK EVERYONE

3. Now for a question on religion. What is your religious preference? IF PROTESTANT, ASK: What Protestant group is that?

   ANGLICAN 1
   UNITED CHURCH 2
   BAPTIST 3
   LUTHERAN 4

   PRESBYTERIAN 5

   OTHER PROTESTANT GROUP 6

   ROMAN CATHOLIC 7
   JEWISH 8
   MOSLEM/HINDU 9

   OTHER (SPECIFY) 1

   NO PREFERENCE 2

BASIC DATA SECTION:

INTERVIEWER: INTRODUCE THIS SECTION AS FOLLOWS:

"Now may I ask you a few questions so that I can be sure I am getting the right sample of people in this community?"

MEN: Are you the **male** head of the household?
WOMEN: Are you the **female** head of the household?

YES . . . . 1 NO 2

ASK EVERYONE:

Are you employed outside the home full-time, part-time or not at all?

FULL-TIME 1
PART-TIME 2
NOT AT ALL 3

ASK EVERYONE:

What is your marital status?

SINGLE 1
MARRIED 2
WID/DIV/SEP 3
LIVING AS MARRIED 4

What was the language you first spoke in childhood and still understand?

ENGLISH 1
FRENCH 2

OTHER (SPECIFY) 3

Now for a question on religion. What is your religious preference — Protestant, Roman Catholic or Jewish?

PROTESTANT 1
JEWISH 2
ROMAN CATHOLIC 3

OTHER (SPECIFY) 4

NO RELIGIOUS PREFERENCE 5

Which of these was the last school that you attended? **HAND CARD "Q"**

Did you graduate from . . . (LEVEL OF SCHOOLING ATTAINED)?
RECORD BELOW

	SOME	GRADUATED
PUBLIC/GRADE SCHOOL	1	2
SECONDARY SCHOOL	3	4
UNIVERSITY	7	8
POST SECONDARY & NON-UNIVERSITY		
COMMUNITY COLLEGE	5	6
C.E.G.E.P.	5	6
OTHER .... (SPECIFY)	5	6
NO FORMAL SCHOOLING	9	
REFUSED	0	

What is your occupation?

SPECIFIC JOB: ....

TYPE OF COMPANY: ....

CHECK IF: ( ) STUDENT
( ) HOUSEWIFE

OCCUPATION OF HEAD OF FAMILY

SPECIFIC JOB? ....

TYPE OF COMPANY?..

How many people, including yourself, are there in this household?

1 2 3 4 5 6 OR MORE

How many would be under 10 years?

0 1 2 3 4 OR MORE

How many would be between 10 & 17 years?

0 1 2 3 4 OR MORE

Are you yourself a member of a trade union, or is your husband/wife a trade union member?

YES, MYSELF 1
YES, MY SPOUSE 2
NO 3

What was the year of your birth?

YEAR . . . .

RECORD IF: MAN . . . . 1 WOMAN 2

HAND CARD "R": Which number on this card corresponds to your total annual family income from all sources before tax deductions?

UNDER $10,000 . . . . 1 $20,000 – $29,999 4
$10,000 – $14,999 . . . . 2 $30,000 – $39,999 5
$15,000 – $19,999 . . . . 3 $40,000 & OVER 6
REFUSED 7

RECORD IF: FARM 1
RURAL, NON-FARM 2
URBAN 3

TIME INTERVIEW ENDED: . . . .

(PLEASE PRINT)

NAME OF RESPONDENT: ____________________

TELEPHONE: ____________________

ADDRESS: ____________________

CITY: ____________________

PROV: ____________________ POSTAL CODE: ____________

DATE OF INTERVIEW: ____________________

I HEREBY ATTEST THAT THIS IS A TRUE AND HONEST INTERVIEW –
INTERVIEWER'S SIGNATURE: ____________________

***A VALIDATION CHECK WILL BE MADE ON ALL INTERVIEWS.

Appendix C

Occupations for Basic Data

Category 1: PROFESSIONAL/TECHNICAL

Accountants/Actuaries/Auditors
Architects
Engineers: Aeronautical
Chemical
Civil
Electrical
Flight
Industrial
Mechanical
Metalurgical
Mining
Petroleum
Sales
Farm & Home Management Advisors
Foresters/Conservationists
Judges/Lawyers
Librarians/Archivists/Curators
Mathematical/Statisticians
Nurses: Registered Nurses
Dieticians
Therapists
Physicians and Related Practitioners: Chiropractors
Dentists
Optometrists
Pharmacists
Veterinarians

Religious Workers: Clergymen
Ministers
Researchers
Scientists: Agricultural
Atmospheric & Space
Biological
Life & Physical
Marine
Chemists
Geologists
Physicists/Astronomers
Chefs
Social
Scientists: Economics
Political/Politicians
Psychologists
Sociologists
Urban & Regional Planners
Teachers/
Instructor: on all levels/vocational & educational counsellors

Technicians & Technologists:
Health; Clinical
Dental Hygenists/Technicians
Health Records, Health
Radiologists/X-ray
Research Technicians
Engineering & Science: Technicians & Technologists: Argricultural
Biological
Chemical
Electrical
Industrial
Mechanical
Other Technicians: Airplane Pilots
Air Traffic Controllers
Embalmers/Undertakers
Writers, Artists and Entertainers: Actors
Athletes
Authors
Dancers
Designers

Editors/Reporters
Musicians & Composers
Painters & Sculptors
Public Relations & Publicity
Producers
Radio & Television Announcers
Morticians
Models
Disc Jockeys

Category 2: BUSINESS EXECUTIVE, OWNERS, MANAGERS & ADMINISTRATORS

Administrators: Health
Public & Local
Ship
Assessors
Brokers
Business Consultants: Architectural
Hardware
Contractors & Builders
Controllers
Construction Inspectors (All Others Code 5)
Dealers
Exporters
Efficiency Experts
Executives
Farmers and Farm Managers (even when working part-time elsewhere)
Funeral Directors
Jobbers
Landlords
Manager of any business (except sales managers & retail trade)
Management Consultants
Manufacturers
Merchants
Nurseryman/Florists
Officials of lodges, societies & unions
Postmasters & Mail Superintendants
Presidents
Property Owners of any business
Publishers

Ship's Officers, Pursers or Pilots
Stock Brokers
Superintendants — if in management position
Treasurers & Secretary Treasurers
Financial Advisors
Planners
Bankers
Co-ordinators
Store Keepers
Expeditors
Developers

Category 3: SALES WORKERS

Advertising Agents
Auctioneers
Commercial Travellers
Demonstrators
Elevator Agents (Grain)
Insurance Agents & Brokers & Underwriters
Manufacturer's Agents
Real Estate Agents & Brokers
Retail Tradespeople
Salesmen & Representatives
Sales Clerks, ie. stores
Sales Managers
Travel Agents

Category 4: CLERICAL WORKERS

Accounting Clerks & Office Clerks: Loans Officers
Payroll & Bookkeepers
Creditman
Timekeepers
Appraisers
Bank Tellers
Cashiers
Clerical Assistants or Supervisors
Collecting Agents — Billing Clerks
Commissioners
Computer Specialists: Programmers
Systems Analysts
Key-punch Operators

Customs Officers
Dispatchers & Radio Operators
Enumerators & Interviewers
Estimators
Insurance Adjusters & Examiners
Real Estate Appraisers
Investigators of all kinds
Inventory Control, Stock Clerks
Library Attendants & Assistants
Meter Readers
Messengers: (Girl or Boy Friday)
Office Machine Operators: Tabulating
Duplicating
Billing & Bookkeeping
Personnel & Labour Relations Workers
Postmen/Women & Postal Clerks
Purchasing Agents & Buyers
Recreation Workers
Shipping & Receiving Clerks
Social & Welfare Workers
Stenographers & Secretaries & Receptionists: Legal, Medical, Private
Teacher's Aides
Telephone & Switchboard Operators
Telegraph Operators & Messengers
Therapy Assistants
Translators
Ticket or Station Agents
Tax Specialists
Production Schedulars
Counsellors
Field Advisors

Category 5: SKILLED LABOR & CRAFTSMEN

Airline Flight Attendants (male or female)
Apprentices of all trades & craftsmen
Armed Forces: (regardless of rank) Army, Navy, Airforce
Asbestos & Installation Workers
Assemblers: Auto-body Builders
Automobile Accessory Installers
Baggage Masters
Bakers

Barbers & Beauty Operators: Hairdressers
Cosmetologists
Bricklayers & Stone Masons: Stone Carvers & Cutters
Butchers & Meat Cutters
Buyers and Shippers for farm products
Carpenters: Cabinetmakers
Furniture & Wood Finishers
Upholsterers
Drywall Installers
Carpet Installers: Floor Layers
Cement & Concrete Finishers
Compositor (Typesetter)
Conductors: Subway, Locomotive, Streetcar, Railroad
Cooks: Saucier, etc.
Decorators: Interior, Window, Paperhangers
Draftsmen
Dressmakers & Milleners: Seamstresses, Tailors, Sewers, Stitchers, Pattern Makers & Cutters
Drivers: Taxi, Truck, Deliverymen, Routemen, Chauffeurs, Bus
Dry Cleaners & Launderers, Presser, Ironers
Electricians
Engineers: Locomotive, Stationery, Audio, Steam Shovel, Radio Transmitting
Engravers
Excavators/Surveyors
Firemen & Fire Protection: Stationary Firemen
Foremen: Supervisors, Farm, Construction, Oil Fields
Furriers
Glaziers (also Lens Grinders & Polishers)
Inspectors: Examiners & Checkers, Manufacturers, Scalers, Graders, Health, Food, Grain, Insurance
Jewellers & Watchmakers (except owners)
Linemen
Lubmermen: Lumberjack, Grader, Logger
Machine Operators: Bulldozer, Heavy Equipment, Back Hoe, Cranemen, Derrickmen, Machinists, Hoistmen, Power Station
Mechanic & Repairmen: Garagemen, Aircraft, Diesel & Heavy Equipment, Farm Equipment, Air Conditioners, Automobiles & Auto Body Repairmen, Office & Data Processing Machines, Household Applicances & Installers, Gasfitters, Radio & TV Repairment

Millers: Grain, Flour, Feed
Millwrights
Movers
Painters (Construction & Maintenance)
Photographic Processors
Plasterers
Plubmers & Pipefitters
Policemen & Detectives: also Sheriffs, Bailiffs, Marshals and Constables
Roofers & Slaters
Sailers & Deck Hands
Sheet Metal Workers: Rollers & Finishers, Structural
Metal Craftsmen
Tinsmiths
Sign Painters & Letterers
Tool & Die Makers & Designers
Trainmen: Trackmen, Brakemen, Firemen, Yardmen
Welders & Solderers
Textile Operators: Knitters, Spinners, Weavers, etc.

Category 6: LABORERS & SERVICE WORKERS

Animal Caretakers
Caretakers of building, stores, etc.
Cleaning Service Workers: Maids
Charwomen, Rooming Housekeepers
Cleaners & Laundresses
Janitors
Maintenance
Carpenter's Helpers
Construction Laborers
Elevators Operators
Factory Workers: Winding Operatives
Miscellaneous Operatives
Seamstresses
Dressmakers
Machine Operators: looms, weavers, sewers
Wrappers & Packers (retail trade)
Fishermen & Oystermen, Seamen
Freight & Material Handlers: Cargomen
Food Service Workers: Bartenders
Busboys
Dishwashers

Food Counter Workers
Waiters & Waitresses

Guards: Doormen
Security Guards
Watchmen
Crossing Guards
Life Guards

Garbage Collectors & Incinerator Workers

Gardeners & Grounds Keepers

Health Service Workers: Dental Assistants
Health Aides
Practical Nurses
Registered Nurses Aid
Hospital Orderly

Laborers and Farm Workers: Stock Handlers

Longshorement: Stevedores

Lumbermen: Raftsmen & Woodchoppers

Miners

Private Household Workers: Child Care Workers
Cooks
Housekeepers, Maids
Servants, Butlers

Section Hands

Stokers

Trappers: Hunters

Warehousemen, Storage Person

Category 7: UNEMPLOYED

(if working part-time, code the occupation)

Category 8: STUDENT

(even if working part-time)

Category 0: OTHER

not in the labor force; disabled, pension; retired (including retired farmers); housewives

REFUSED, DID NOT STATE

Year of Birth — Below 1901, code as 98
Refused, code as 99

Appendix D

Christianity as a Source of Anti-Judaism

Parkes, Ruether, Davies, Baum, Baker, Bishop and other scholars of Christian theology and church history have written extensively on the role of Christianity in the emergence of anti-Jewish prejudice. The central theme of this scholarship was expressed well in the preface to an anthology entitled *AntiSemitism and the Foundations of Christianity* and edited by University of Toronto Professor Alan Davies. Professor Davies wrote that

> the scholars represented in these pages wish to extract Christianity from what the Canadian poet Irving Layton has styled "Xianity": that false and evil religion that has bred *Judenhass* and murder for centuries, and which must now be exorcised once and for all:
>
> Come back to us, Jeshua;
> cast out the devil of Jew-hatred
> in Xian and goy,
> heal them of an ancient sickness.[1]

Published in 1979, *AntiSemitism and the Foundations of Christianity* was dedicated to the Rev. James Parkes on his 80th birthday.

A Church of England clergyman and scholar of religious history, Parkes wrote countless books and pamphlets during the more than fifty years which he devoted to improved Jewish-Christian relations and heightened Christian self-understanding. In the period leading up to the Holocaust, Parkes was anxious to show that the secular stories about Jews' poisoning wells, causing disease, killing Jewish children for Passover, spying on Christian governments, controlling international finance, manipulating world politics and so forth had their roots in Christian theology and not in secular reality. In 1934, he first published his heavily documented review of the first eight centuries of Christian-Jewish relations entitled *The Conflict of the Church and the Synagogue: The Origins of Antisemitism.*[2] Parkes reported finding mammoth evidence of religiously inspired hostility to Jews in this period but virtually no trace of secularly inspired hatred. Indeed, he found much more evidence of economic and social dislike of Greeks and Egyptians than of Jews. Parkes identified the clear origins of Nazi ideas about Jews' being agents of Satan and destroyers of Christian civilization in the Christian sermons of the 4th century and earlier.[3]

Dr. Parkes reviewed at great length the nature and origins of the many decrees limiting the life of Jews, for example those which made it a capital offence to rest on Saturday, the Jewish sabbath, or a capital offence to convert or to help someone to convert to Judaism. He concluded that "almost all the legislation affecting the Jews comes from those kings who were in close alliance with, or the tools of, the clerical party...".[4] He also noted that "it was those who were popular with the common people who passed no measures against the Jews, or allowed them to evade the restrictions of their predecessors; whereas it was those who were allied to the ecclesiastical and noble parties who most violently oppressed them."[5]

In his prolific writing, the Rev. Parkes always emphasized the Christian origins of anti-Judaism but did not always pinpoint exactly the same facet of Christianity. In some instances, Parkes attributed anti-Judaism to the growing frustrations of the early Church with the persistent popularity of the older religion and with the refusal of Jews to see the light. The Church needed to demonologize Juaism in order to explain the resistance of Jews to its message. After all, Jesus himself was a devout Jew. In some instances, Parkes pointed directly to the *Gospels* as the problem.

Parkes not only surveyed anti-Judaism in the distant past but also examined the modern "anti-semitic" movements in 19th and 20th century Europe. From his detailed analysis of even the modern movements, Parkes concluded that clerics played a prominent role in "all" of them.[6] Individual clerics were often in leadership positions while the national Church helped to furnish legitimacy for the attack on Jews.

Parkes inspired many other scholars of religious history, including the American Catholic theologian Rosemary Radford Ruether. Her book *Faith and Fratricide* and her considerable other writing on the subject have caused quite a stir. She argued that anti-Judaism was the "lefthand" of Christianity:

> It was Christian theology that developed the thesis of the reprobate status of the Jew in history and laid the foundations of the demonic view of the Jew that fanned the flames of popular hatred. This hatred was not only inculcated by Christian preaching and exegesis. It became incorporated into the structure of canon law and also the civil law formed under the Christian Roman emperors...These anti-Judaic laws of the church and the Christian empire laid the basis for the debasement of

the civic and personal status of the Jew in Christian society that lasted until the emancipation in the nineteenth century. These laws were, in part, revived in the Nazi Nuremberg Laws of 1933.[7]

Outside the English-speaking world, the most influential scholar of religious history on this question was Jules Isaac. A highly decorated veteran of World War I, Isaac became a respected scholar of secular history and was appointed Inspector General of Education for France. After the Nazi invasion of 1940, he felt obliged to confront the issue of the sources of anti-Judaism. While moving from hiding place to hiding place, he wrote the classic *Jesus and Israel*. He identified and argued against 21 factual errors in Christian teachings which led to the denigration of Judaism. He pointed out that Jesus was an observant Jew from a Jewish family and taught in a vibrant Jewish setting. He dealt at great length with the accusation of deicide. According to Isaacs, even if it is proper to blame Jews today for what the Jewish people are thought to have done 19 centuries ago, and even if Jews under Roman governors and military occupation can somehow be held solely responsible for the crucifixion, the fact remains that most Jews did not participate in the crucifixion. Most Jews were not even aware of Jesus' existence, dispersed as they were in the far-flung diaspora. *Jesus and Israel* concluded with a program of action for changing Christian teachings. The book provoked a crisis of conscience.

Jules Isaac assembled a distinguished body of Roman Catholic and Jewish clergy and scholars in Seelisberg, Switzerland to hammer out a program for reforming Christian liturgy in order to purify it of anti-Jewish anomosity. The Seelisberg program became a catalyst for reform within the Roman Church. French catechisms and textbooks underwent revision.[8] During the early 1960's, the Second Vatican Council declared that Jews would henceforth not be considered responsible for the death of Jesus and that blaming Jews for the death should be roundly condemned. Rome reached this decision in the face of vigorous political pressure by Arab governments to retain the traditional interpretation.[9]

Easter has often been problematic for Christian-Jewish relations. In the medieval period, some Western European churches included the ceremonial beating of an individual Jew as part of the service. Under Czarist rule, Russians Jews often contended with pogroms or massacres following the Easter sermon. The Roman Catholic liturgy for Good Friday included special prayers or intercessions including one for the Pope, one for the Church, one for Jews, and one for nonbelievers. For more than a thousand years, each of the intercessions except the one for Jews was accompanied by a silent prayer on bended knee. But, this practice was reformed in 1955, partly in response to Isaac's efforts.[10] In 1958, Pope John XXIII removed the word "perfidious" from the title of the prayer for Jews."

The formal Roman Catholic liturgy for Good Friday also includes a special prayer which is directed against Jews and which is known as the improperia or reproaches. In Roman liturgy, the reproaches are said to be the words of Jesus on the cross.[11] The text reads in part as follows:

> My people what have I done to you?
> How have I offended you? Answer me!
>
> I led you out of Egypt, from slavery to freedom,
> but you led your Savior to the cross.
>
> My people, what have I done to you?
> How have I offended you? Answer me!

The full text of the reproaches appears in the end of this appendix. Today, many parish priests in English-speaking Canada do not use this prayer in active service. But, in many parts of the world, especially the Third World, its use is obligatory.

The principal Protestant denominations do not appear to have anything directly comparable to the reproaches said to have been uttered by Jesus in Roman liturgy. According to Lutheran theology, Jesus could not have uttered those words since Lutherans hold that Jesus died without a murmur on behalf of humankind. Some Protestant denominations have had special prayers calling explicitly for the conversion of Jews. For example, the 1918 prayer book of the Anglican Church of Canada implored God to "Have mercy upon the Jews, thine ancient people, and upon all who reject and deny thy Son; take from them all ignorance, hardness of heart and contempt of thy word; and so fetch them home...that they may be saved among the remnant of the true Israelites..." The current prayer book (1959) no longer describes Christians as the "true Israelites." In 1965, the Church decided to omit the prayer from actual use, a decision which was subsequently reaffirmed on several occasions. The new book in preparation will apparently contain no such prayer.[12] In 1983, the Anglican synod decided to introduce Holocaust curricula into Sunday school teaching. The Church has also made a special effort to persuade provincial Education Ministries to develop Holocaust curricula. Several Anglican clergy have been in the forefront of Jewish-Christian reconciliation.[13]

The Reproaches

In Roman Catholic Liturgy For Good Friday

My people, what have I done to you?
How have I offended you? Answer me!

I led you out of Egypt, from slavery to freedom,
but you led your Savior to the cross.

Holy is God!

Holy and strong!

Holy immortal One,
have mercy on us!

For forty years, I led you safely through the desert.
I fed you with manna from heaven
and brought you to a land of plenty;
but you led your Savior to the cross.

Holy is God!

Holy and strong!

Holy immortal One,
have mercy on us!

What more could I have done for you?
I planted you as my fairest vine,
but you yielded only bitterness:
when I was thirsty you gave me vinegar to drink,
and you pierced your Savior with a lance.

Holy is God!

Holy and strong!

Holy immortal One,
have mercy on us!

For your sake I scourged your captors and their firstborn sons,
but you brought your scourges down on me.

My people what have I done to you?
How have I offended you? Answer me!

I led you from slavery to freedom
and drowned your captors in the sea,
but you handed me over to your high priests.

My people, what have I done to you?
How have I offended you? Answer me!

I opened the sea before you,
but you opened my side with a spear.

My people, what have I done to you?
How have I offended you? Answer me!

I led you on your way in a pillar of cloud,
but you led me to Pilate's court.

My people, what have I done to you?
How have I offended you? Answer me!

I bore you up with manna in the desert,
but you struck me down and scourged me.

My people, what have I done to you?
How have I offended you? Answer me!

I gave you saving water from the rock,
but you gave me gall and vinegar to drink.

My people, what have I done to you?
How have I offended you? Answer me!

For you I struck down the Kings of Canaan,
but you struck my head with a reed.

My people, what have I done to you?
How have I offended you? Answer me!

I gave you a royal scepter,
but you have me a crown of thorns.

My people, what have I done to you?
How have I offended you? Answer me!

I raised you to the height of majesty,
but you raised me high on a cross.

My people, what have I done to you?
How have I offended you? Answer me!

[1] Alan T. Davies, *AntiSemitism and the Foundations of Christianity: Twelve Christian Theologians Explore the Development and Dynamics of AntiSemitism within the Christian Tradition* (New York: Paulist Press, 1979), xvii. The poetic excerpt is from Irving Layton, "The Exorcist," *The Covenant* (Toronto: McClelland and Stewart, 1977). See also Alan T. Davies, *Antisemitism and the Christian Mind: The Crisis of Conscience after Auschwitz* (Toronto, 1969). Professor Davies and Carleton University Professor Steve Wilson are editing a momentous two volume work on the Christian sources of anti-Judaism to be published in late 1985 and in 1986 by Wilfrid Laurier University Press.

[2] Reprinted by Atheneum (New York, 1974).

[3] Throughout *The Conflict of the Church and Synagogue* and also in James Parkes, *Anti-Semitism: a Concise World History* (Chicago: Quadrangle Books, 1963) chap. V, "The Christian Roots of Anti-Semitism."

[4] *The Conflict of the Church and Synagogue*, p. 348.

[5] *ibid.*, p. 349.

[6] From James Parkes' preface (p. vi) to Alan T. Davies, ed., *AntiSemitism and the Foundations of Christianity.* See also James Parkes, *The Emergence of the Jewish Problem, 1878-1939* (Westport, Conn.: Greenwood Press, 1970).

[7] Rosemary Radford Ruether, "Christology and Jewish-Christian Relations" in Abraham J. Peck, ed., *Jews and Christians after the Holocaust* (Philadelphia: Fortress Press, 1982), p. 25.

[8] See the forword by Claire Huchet Bishop to Jules Isaac, *Jesus and Israel* (New York: Holt, Rinehart and Winston, 1971).

[9] "Declaration on the Relationship of the Church to Non-Christian Religions" in Herbert Vorgrimler, ed., *Commentary on the Documents of Vatican II* (New York: Herder and Herder, 1969) and Franklin H. Littell, *The Crucifixion of the Jews* (New York: Harper and Row, 1975), p. 28.

[10] See Claire Huchet Bishop's introduction to Jules Isaac, *The Teaching of Contempt: Christian Roots of Anti-Semitism* (Chicago: Holt, Rinehart, and Winston, 1964) and Gregory Baum, *Is the New Testament Anti-Semitic?* (New York: Paulist Press, 1965), pp. 24-5.

[11] "The reproaches... appear... as utterances of Jesus during the Adoration of the Cross in the Roman liturgy of Good Friday." *New Catholic Encyclopedia,* Volume 7, p. 407, "Improperia."

[12]Written communication from the Rev. Brian Prideaux, Ecumenical Officer, Anglican Church of Canada, summer, 1985.

[13] The best known of these is the Liberal M.P., Rev. Roland de Corneille, who was once an official of the League for Human Rights of B'nai Brith. See his *Christians and Jews: Dialogue (Toronto: Longmans, 1966).* Another example is the Rev. Canon William Gilbert, Director of Program for the Anglican Diocese of Ottawa. In the Church of England, a major figure is Bishop John Austen Baker. See his anthology, *Theology and Racism: The Bible, Racism, and Anti-Semitism* (London: Church of England, 1985).

Index